Acquisition Essentials

FT Prentice Hall
FINANCIAL TIMES

In an increasingly competitive world, we believe it's
quality of thinking that gives you the edge – an idea that
opens new doors, a technique that solves a problem, or an
insight that simply makes sense of it all. The more you
know, the smarter and faster you can go.

That's why we work with the best minds in business
and finance to bring cutting-edge thinking
and best learning practice to a global market.

Under a range of leading imprints, including
Financial Times Prentice Hall, we create world-class
print publications and electronic products bringing our
readers knowledge, skills and understanding, which can
be applied whether studying or at work.

To find out more about Pearson Education publications,
or tell us about the books you'd like to find, you can
visit us at **www.pearsoned.co.uk**

PEARSON
Education

Acquisition Essentials

A step-by-step guide to smarter deals

Denzil Rankine
Peter Howson

FT Prentice Hall
FINANCIAL TIMES

An imprint of Pearson Education

Harlow, England • London • New York • Boston • San Francisco • Toronto • Sydney • Singapore • Hong Kong
Tokyo • Seoul • Taipei • New Delhi • Cape Town • Madrid • Mexico City • Amsterdam • Munich • Paris • Milan

PEARSON EDUCATION LIMITED

Edinburgh Gate
Harlow, CM20 2JE
Tel: +44 (0)1279 623623
Fax: +44 (0)1279 431059
Website: www.pearsoned.co.uk

First published in Great Britain in 2006

ISBN-13: 978-0-273-68861-7
ISBN-10: 0-273-68861-8

British Library Cataloguing-in-Publication Data
A catalogue record for this book is available from the British Library

Library of Congress Cataloging-in-Publication Data
A catalog record for this book is available from the Library of Congress

10 9 8 7 6 5 4 3 2 1
10 09 08 07 06

Typeset in 9.5pt/13pt New Century Schoolbook by 30
Printed in Great Britain by Henry Ling Ltd., at the Dorset Press, Dorchester, Dorset
The publisher's policy is to use paper manufactured from sustainable forests.

About the authors

Denzil Rankine is chief executive of AMR International, which he founded in 1991. He has grown the business to become a world leading market and strategic due diligence specialist, based in London, Frankfurt and New York.

Denzil has 20 years' experience of advising companies on acquisitions and strategic development. After his early career in the US he has worked on many hundreds of acquisition programmes with European and American acquirers.

Denzil has advised on agreed and hostile acquisitions and private equity transactions with values ranging up to $2 bn. This work has taken him to 33 different countries.

Denzil is the author of four M&A related books: *A Practical Guide to Acquisitions* (Wiley), *Commercial Due Diligence – a guide to reducing risk in acquisitions* (Financial Times Prentice Hall), *Why Acquisitions Fail* (Financial Times Prentice Hall) and *Due Diligence* (Financial Times Prentice Hall).

Peter Howson is a director of AMR International, London's leading Commercial Due Diligence specialist. Peter has over 20 years of M&A and business development experience both in industry and as an adviser. Before joining AMR in 1998 Peter worked in corporate finance at Barings where he focused on domestic and cross border deals in manufacturing industries. Prior to that he was part of the small team which, through 75 acquisitions and disposals, transformed TI Group, a UK PLC, from a domestic manufacturer of mainly commodity products into a global engineering company focused on specialist niche markets. He has also held senior finance and M&A roles with British Steel and T&N. He is a qualified accountant and has an MBA from Manchester Business School.

Publisher's acknowledgements

The original versions of the following appear in *Due Diligence* by Denzil Rankine, Mark Bomer and Graham Stedman, FT Prentice Hall, 2003:

Case Study 5.1 – Ferranti; Figure 5.1 'The acquisition process'; Figure 5.2 'The commercial due diligence process'; Figure 5.2 'Primary information sources'; Table 5.2 'A CDD report format'; Table 5.3 'Different key purchase criteria amongst customers of removals firms'; Table 5.4 'Relationship between KPCs, CSFs and KPIs in the bicycle market'; Figure 5.6 'How CDD and FDD combine to build a view of forecasts'; Appendix A 'Checklist for a financial due diligence investigation'; Appendix C 'Checklist for legal due diligence'.

In some instances we have been unable to trace the owners of copyright material, and we would appreciate any information that would enable us to do so.

Contents

Appendices

Executive summary

Acquisition Essentials provides a step-by-step approach to getting acquisitions right.

This practical guide is an invaluable tool for any business or organisation looking to expand its operations through the acquisition of companies. The book outlines why acquisitions fail and how to get them right through every stage of the acquisition process: from the planning stage of how to find candidates and gives practical guidance on carrying out preliminary negotiations and due diligence investigations. It also provides invaluable realistic advice on valuations and negotiations and concludes by explaining how to draft the sales and purchase agreement and manage post-acquisition integration. The book also contains a number of useful checklists and case studies to guide would-be acquirers through the whole process to a successful conclusion.

Foreword

Acquisition decisions are not like other decisions. In Chapter 1, Denzil and Peter point out that 'most acquisitions fail', and these are normally the main words of caution to managers. However, decisions with low success rates are familiar to most managers. Think of new product launches or management appointments or IT investments. Against these comparisons, success rates of 30–50 per cent seem quite normal. So the special feature of acquisitions is not their low success rate. The special feature is that acquisition decisions involve big stakes and small prizes.

In most decisions, such as a new product launch, managers make an investment of a few million and, if the decision succeeds, expect to reap returns five or ten times the investment. Of course, a percentage of the time the investment fails; but the failures are paid for by the successes: one success can usually support three or four failures. With acquisitions the sums are different.

In an acquisition the buyer normally pays full value for the target company plus a premium. In other words the buyer pays the discounted value of all future cash flows from the business, plus 10–50 per cent more. The reason why buyers pay premiums is important to understand. They pay premiums because they are normally in competition with other buyers and because they often need to pay a premium to persuade the seller to sell.

The prize is the value of the business after it has been improved by and integrated with its new owners less the total amount paid to the seller and spent on the deal and integration process. If the premium is 30 per cent, a number that Denzil and Peter consider normal, and the value of the business after it has been improved and integrated is 150 per cent of its value before acquisition, the prize is 20 per cent. In other words, the buyer has spent 130 per cent for a prize of 20 per cent: a decision of big stakes and small prizes.

In this situation – a stake of 130 and a prize of 20 – the successes are unlikely to pay for the failures. One bad decision can lose the buyer 100 which will only be recouped by 5 good decisions. The economics of acquisition decisions are, therefore, very different from the economics of most other decisions that managers get involved in.

It is this problem that I focus on in my teaching of acquisition strategy. How should managers approach a decision where the stakes are big, the prizes are small, there are high degrees of uncertainty about valuations and about integration synergies and the premium a buyer has to pay is driven by the amount competing buyers are willing to pay?

I have distilled my guidance into a number of rules:

Rule 1: Do not acquire with cash during an acquisition boom

At five times during the last century there have been more buyers of companies than sellers. These boom periods – the last two were at the end of the 1980s and 1990s – coincide with unreasonably high stock market prices and hence unrealistically high valuations. Managers who pay with cash during these periods will over pay and commit themselves and their successors to work hard in order to stand still.

The best policy is to avoid acquisitions during acquisition booms. However, some strategies cannot wait until the stock market comes to its senses. These deals should be paid for with shares. If managers use shares to make acquisitions when they think prices are high, they will be buying expensive paper and paying with expensive paper, passing on the overpricing risk to the shareholders of the selling company.

Rule 2: The improvements and synergies need to be greater than the premium

Denzil and Peter make this point in Chapter 1. There is no prize unless the integration plan creates improvements and synergies bigger than the premium. In fact the only time that the prize is likely to be big is when the improvements and synergies are large compared to the value of the company as a stand-alone business. If the improvements and synergies are 100 per cent or 200 per cent, the prize will be large even with a premium of 50 per cent.

There is one exception to this rule – when the target company is selling for a discount. While these situations do exist, buyers should beware of discounts. No price is low enough when buying a business that routinely destroys value.

Rule 3: The improvements and synergies we can create need to be bigger than the improvements and synergies rival bidders can create

This is a tough hurdle. But the logic is sound. Since the premium is determined by the price that the next highest bidder is prepared to pay, we should be cautious outbidding someone who can create more improvements and synergies than us. Lets take an example. If we can create synergies of 30 per cent and another company can create synergies of 50 per cent, this other company can afford to pay 20 per cent more than us.

The problem is that neither buyer is able to accurately value the target as a stand-alone business or value the size of the improvements and synergies. This is because both valuations depend on forecasts of the future. This means that we will only win the bidding if we are more than 20 per cent overoptimistic and the rival bidder is realistic or if we are realistic and the rival bidder is more than 20 per cent pessimistic. Since it is hard for us to know whether we are being optimistic or pessimistic and even harder to guess the mindset of the rival bidders, we are better off not outbidding a company that can create more improvements and synergies than us.

Rule 4: Don't forget learning costs and distraction costs

The equation is not just:

prize = synergies less premium

The equation is:

Prize = synergies less premium less learning costs less distraction costs less deal costs

The less familiar the new business, the higher the learning costs. This is why diversification decisions are less successful than deals in the core business. Learning costs are hard to estimate because they come mainly from the mistakes managers make when they are in unfamiliar markets. In my experience, learning costs are rarely less than 10 per cent and can be as high as 50 per cent of the value of the target company if it is an unfamiliar market.

Distraction costs are driven by the loss of management attention to existing businesses. Each acquisition needs to be assessed for its distraction impact. How many managers will be involved in the acquisition and what would they otherwise have been doing? If the acquisition is likely to draw significant attention from existing businesses, it can easily lead to a loss of value in these businesses of 10–30 per cent.

Frequently, when managers do the maths for the full equation, a prize of 20 per cent quickly evaporates under the burden of 10 per cent learning costs, significant distraction costs and deal costs that often amount to more than 5 per cent.

Rule 5: The prize from an acquisition needs to be greater than the prize from a joint venture or alliance with the target company (assuming these are available)

Since the full equation often results in situations with big synergies looking as though they will only produce a small, rather risky, prize, it is often better to go for the synergies through a joint venture or an alliance. When the target is determined to sell, this lower risk solution may not be available. Nevertheless, it is important to assess whether the prize from a joint venture or alliance (no premium, reduced learning costs and lower deal costs) is likely to be greater. If so, it may be better not to bid for the target company and instead form an alliance with one of its competitors. As Denzil and Peter explain, acquisitions are usually a last resort.

Using these five rules is hard. They stop most deals. Hyperactive managers are usually uncomfortable, arguing that the rules are too pessimistic or that there are defensive reasons for deals that cannot be assessed through the 'synergies less premium' equation. However, the rules are based on simple logic and simple mathematics. Ignore them at your peril.

Andrew Campbell
Director, Ashridge Strategic
Management Centre

The foundations 1

Acquisitions are a powerful strategic tool that can be used to grow and even transform companies. However, they are not a quick fix for operational, strategic or even financial problems. As we shall see in this book, acquisition can be a risky business. Because of the dangers, acquirers need to ensure that they are using them for the right strategic reasons and that they carefully manage the whole acquisition process. It is too easy for the deal to become a goal in itself. Essential, complex questions can end up being dismissed as irrelevant, boring or too mundane to be answered properly. This would not happen when installing a new machine or a new IT system, and it should not happen with acquisitions, but buying a company is a high profile, ego driven, activity in which hordes of people have a vested interest in the deal going ahead. I still remember with a shudder the corporate financier from a large New York investment bank telling us that, 'this was a great deal' just after we had discovered uninsured asbestos liabilities.

As the buyer, you have to live with the consequences of a bad deal for many years. To minimise your chances of failure, you should understand why so many of them fail and so draw up your acquisition plan to avoid the more obvious pitfalls.

Bad news...most acquisitions fail

It is hard to provide a perfect measure of acquisition success or failure, particularly as subsequent events and management actions often muddy the waters. As shown in Table 1.1 overleaf, numerous studies have shown that most acquisitions fail.

Planning for success

Success depends on avoiding mistakes in any phase of the acquisition process from the initial planning through to well after the businesses have been combined. The five key phases of an acquisition are:

- Strategic and acquisition planning
- Acquisition target evaluation
- Deal management

Table 1.1	Surveys showing that acquisitions do not always add value			
Source	*Sample*	*Time frame*	*Percentage failed*	*Measurement*
Mitchell/EIU	150	1988–1996	70%	Would not buy again (self assessment)
Coopers & Lybrand	125	Completed 1996	66%	Revenues, cash flow, profitability
Mercer Management	215	Completed 1997	48%	Share price relative to industry index after three years
McKinsey	193	1990–1997	65–70%	Industry specific benchmarks
Arthur Andersen	Large mergers in time period	1994–1997	44%	Methods not fully described
Booz-Allen & Hamilton	NA	1997–1998	53%	Methods not fully described
Arthur Andersen	31 technology, media and entertainment companies	2000	63%	Negative impacts: management difficulties, distraction from other businesses etc
Sirower BCG	302	1995–2001	61%	Share price relative to S&P 500
AT Kearny	25,000	1988–2001	50%	Share price relative to industry index
KPMG	122	2000–2001	31%	Share price relative to industry index

- Integration management
- Corporate development

There are four factors to look out for in each phase.

Strategic and acquisition planning

Have you sufficient strength to be acquiring?

If you had the 'flu, would you run a marathon? Clearly not. The same is true for companies planning to acquire. Any company must start an acquisition programme from firm foundations. Acquisitions consume an enormous amount of management time and other resources. The existing business has to be running well enough to sustain the strain of buying and integrating another one. Acquisitions divert attention from challenges in the core business. For example Compaq was facing intensifying competition in its core PC market when it acquired Digital, which was also facing tough competition in its markets. The combined businesses struggled to integrate and their combined performance was unexciting.

Do you have the right strategy?

As already noted, acquisitions are a strategic tool. This means that, before buying another company, the acquirer needs a clear strategy in which an acquisition can be shown to add value. For example AT&T decided to enter the IT arena in the early 1990s looking for the expected benefits of the convergence of IT and telephony. It acquired NCR in 1991 for $7.5 bn – a company which it shoehorned into its strategy. The fit was poor and, worse, NCR was not an IT company but a supplier of cash registers that happened to use IT. AT&T divested the company in 1995 making a loss of more than $3.5 bn on the transaction.

Numerous companies pursued flawed strategies at the time of the dotcom boom, mainly because they understood neither the fundamentals of the Net nor, more surprisingly, of their own businesses. Time Warner's merger with AOL was among the most spectacular. Time Warner was not able to dramatically increase the revenues earned by its content because it also owned an Internet Service Provider (ISP). Having the right strategy means understanding how the acquirer can add value, for example through top line growth or by taking out cost. Figure 1.1 overleaf compares the acquisition strategies applicable to different growth strategies.

Fig 1.1 Various growth strategies require acquisitions

Growth strategy comparison

Strategy	Growth method	Top line growth	Improved pricing	Cost savings	Examples
Build-up	Small acquisitions	✓✓✓✓	✓	✓✓	Nursing homes
Consolidation	Selective large acquisitions	✓✓	✓✓	✓✓✓	Pharmaceutical industry, steel producers
'Missing link'	Selective large acquisitions	✓✓✓	✓✓✓✓	✓	Vodafone/ Mannesman
Roll-out	Small start-ups	✓✓✓✓	✗	✓	Coffee shops

Key: extent to which benefit is delivered

✗ not at all ——→ ✓✓✓✓ fully

Source: AMR International

Do not make opportunistic acquisitions

If a company has sensibly defined acquisition as a realistic and sensible growth path, the lack of availability of the right acquisition target is a major frustration. But one of the worst reasons to select an acquisition is simply because it happens to be available.

The economics of Mergers and Acquisitions (M&A) are very simple. Unless you have impeccable inside information, you will end up paying at least 30 per cent more than a business is actually worth. To make a success of an acquisition, therefore, you have to be able to add value at least equal to that premium. To do this you must be able to bring something new. Do you really expect to be able to do this with a business which just happens to come up? I remember sitting open-mouthed when the disgruntled financial controller of a very large UK engineering company told me how disillusioned he had become with his bosses because their acquisition strategy consisted of 'buying companies on the cheap that they think they can turn round, failing and selling them off a couple of years later at a loss'. As the one who had to pick up the financial pieces there was no wonder he was frustrated.

All serial acquirers tend to come unstuck in the end. One example in the 1980s and 1990s was ITT. It created a broad group with interests ranging from hotels to telephone directories to pumps. In reality, the deal-doing frenzy did not create value; the group became unwieldy and then paid the price for its lack of acquisition rationale as management failed to exploit the group's assets.

In the late 1990s some private equity investors engaged in 'drive-by investing': they hardly stopped long enough to see what they were backing. Rentokil promised a 20 per cent annual growth to the city and found itself making bigger and less logical acquisitions. The acquisition of BET in 1996 was the start of its undoing as Rentokil was unable to dramatically improve what BET was doing.

Consider the alternatives

As such a risky business development tool, acquisition can be seen as a last resort. Toyota entered the luxury car market successfully through Lexus. In contrast Ford, which paid a premium for Jaguar, subsequently faced high integration costs and found that its cost per car was much higher. As a company seeks to grow it should not immediately leap to the conclusion that it must acquire to achieve its goal. It must decide whether the natural advantages of acquisition which are speed, scale and bringing specific assets or skills, outweigh the risks.

Acquisition target evaluation

Understand the market

An acquirer needs a complete understanding of both its own and the target company's market and how it proposes to use the target to develop. It needs to know what drives the market, what is happening within it, how it will evolve and how the profitability of participants will evolve. A common mistake made by acquirers is to assume that they 'know' the market because they already operate in it. If the target business is in an adjacent segment, the acquirer's assumptions can be positively dangerous. EMAP entered the French publishing market through a joint venture with Bayard Presse and developed subsequently by launching its own titles before finally acquiring a leading publisher, Editions Mondial. The architect of the strategy then went on to open up the US by acquiring Peterson for £932 m. With no local knowledge and too much confidence the deal was a disaster.

Dot.com investors and traditional businesses that acquired new economy start-ups misjudged the market dramatically. People often overestimate the impact of new technologies in the short term, but underestimate it in the long term.

It is also important to work out why the business is really for sale. The seller may have spotted a problem looming in the market. This is particularly true of entrepreneurs who are good at sensing when a business has reached its full potential. In the early 1980s, Reynolds Rings, a UK subsidiary of the British engineering company TI Group, bought King Fifth Wheel (KFW) in the USA. Reynolds made engine rings, the structural outer casing of jet engines. It used a process which is best described as sophisticated blacksmithing. This comprised of heating a long slab of exotic steel, bending it into a ring and flash-butt welding the join between the two ends. The fabricated ring then spent several months in a sub-contract machine shop having all the holes, wells and channels machined into it from which would hang the engine's subsystems and fuel lines. Reynolds biggest customer was the UK jet engine manufacturer Rolls Royce. KFW made exactly the same product in exactly the same way. Its biggest customer was the number two US jet engine maker Pratt and Whitney.

On paper this was a marriage made in heaven. Buying KFW would give Reynolds access to the lucrative US market on a scale which would give it an R&D advantage over its rivals in the US and Europe. It did the deal without any market due diligence. After the deal was done TI insisted (rather late in the day) that Reynolds come up with a development plan. A colleague was dispatched to research the American market. His first stop was a meeting with the R&D director at Pratt and Whitney. He soon made it clear why KFW and indeed the other four other rings makers in the US were for sale. There was a new technology coming along which allowed most of the machining to be done pre-forming, which was considerably cheaper and quicker.

Understand the target's business model

Understanding the market is one thing, understanding the target's business model is another. As an acquirer, do you really understand why this business you are going to buy makes money? Different companies in the same market make money in different ways and for different reasons. In air travel, BA focuses on service, Ryanair on price; in computing, Dell focuses on delivery, Compaq on quality. Club Med makes money from its packages, resort hotels make money from the extras. These are the obvious examples, differences between businesses are often more subtle.

Acquirers need to challenge their initial assumptions and make time to understand how the target operates; this means understanding how it generates its revenues and where the best margins lie. This analysis should also show where it could be losing out. The financial information on the business will provide the initial pointers, but an acquirer needs to understand far more. What are the processes, people and other resources that allow the company to achieve what it does? Gaining this understanding is essential because otherwise the acquirer can unwittingly make changes which damage the performance of the business. Without a comprehensive assessment of how, and how far, the target will be integrated into the new joint operation the acquirer can work out where the operational and business development gains are to be achieved.

In the engine rings example above, one of the chief reasons KFW did so much business with Pratt and Whitney was the personal relationship between KFW's president and an important vice-president at Pratt. The last thing that needed to happen post acquisition was for him to be fired or moved.

Work out synergies early on

At an early stage of the process an acquirer needs to justify – in detail – the synergies it hopes to achieve. Logically it should never be otherwise, but often is. It is all too tempting to adjust some of the up-sides of an acquisition when modelling its future performance to get a desired number in the total box of your spreadsheet. The market for companies is highly competitive. Synergies justify the price you will have to pay, so how can you go into price negotiations without having worked out where they are going to come from and when and how you are going to release them?

The acquirer must base its synergy estimates on evidence, benchmarks and directly relevant experience, not just assumptions. Cost reduction synergies are the safest: they are typically relatively easy to quantify and deliver and the finance director will believe your sums. The danger is that you make changes which damage the business because you did not understand the business model. For example Wells Fargo, the US bank, acquired First Interstate Bank for its high-net-worth customers. Its attempt to achieve cost reduction synergies (through branch closures and a reduction in service levels) destroyed any hope of achieving the predicted business development gains, because it could not serve First Interstate's wealthy customers in the manner they expected.

Sales growth synergies are much harder to quantify and achieve. Sales forces do not always work well together; customers do not fall over themselves to buy more products from the company which just bought their supplier. Many of the sales synergies which are modelled in acquisition cases are illusory. However, perhaps they deserve more attention because there is a large body of evidence that suggests that cost reductions are short-lived while sales gains are critical to successful acquisitions.[1]

Identification of problem areas in due diligence

A key purpose of due diligence is to identify the big problem areas and the black holes. Ferranti, the well-respected British defence giant would not have bankrupted itself by buying ISC, another electronics company had it conducted commercial due diligence (CDD) and spoken to a few (non-existent) customers instead of just relying on the seller's word, management opinion and a re-hashed audit. British & Commonwealth hit the rocks over the Atlantic computers leasing liabilities, which proper project management of due diligence would have picked up. Cendant shot itself in the foot by skimping on financial due diligence in its acquisition of HFS and Comp-U-Card 'CUC'.

But due diligence is not just about finding problems. As we will see in Chapter 5 (Investigating the target) it should also be used to identify and quantify the potential synergies and feed in to the integration actions needed to unlock them. The quality of due diligence has improved dramatically over the past 20 years as acquirers have sought to avoid the mistakes of others but it is still, wrongly, seen as the boring bit of deal-doing.

Deal management

If you do not manage the deal process effectively you increase the risk of a fatal result. The acquisition team needs to be well prepared and to retain control of its process and its emotions.

Right price

There is no such thing as a right price for an acquisition; a company is worth what the buyer is prepared to pay. This is shown by the William Low example[2]. By launching a counter bid for the Scottish retailer William Low, Sainsbury forced Tesco to react and to pay £93 m (60 per cent) more than the price origi-nally agreed by both sides. In the end Tesco paid William Low's shareholders what it thought the business was worth which was far above the shareholders' initially accepted valuation.

Corporate finance advisers now ensure that most companies are sold at auc-tion, with a range of competing bidders. Buyers must set a walk-away price based on a realistic valuation. Experienced acquirers will testify that having walked away on price, the same deal often comes back a few years later.

Do not 'wing' the negotiations

Significant amounts of value can be won and lost in negotiation. Anyone who has been on a negotiating course is well aware from the practical examples of the discrepancy between what the sellers are prepared to accept and what buy-ers are prepared to pay. An acquirer needs to have the right negotiating team which has done its homework, excellent communication within the team and a clear negotiation strategy. Do not jet in the other board member for the photo opportunity at the final signing ceremony unless the details are all tied down. Otherwise the other side will hold you to ransom whilst your increasingly impa-tient colleagues ask what is going on.

Prepare well

An acquisition process is rarely straightforward. Each deal has its own twists and complications. The level of time and resources required can be a shock to those unfamiliar with acquisitions. Before embarking on an acquisition, the acquirer needs to ensure that all the necessary internal and external processes and relationships are in place. If internal approvals are not in place, the process can become so bogged down that a rival buyer slips in to woo a frustrated target.

You also need controls. Whilst an acquisition requires a champion to push it through and for it to succeed, it is essential for balancing controls to be in place. If they are not, deal fever can take over and an acquisition, however poor, can become unstoppable.

Frustrations and problems with the process are not all self-inflicted. Target companies and their advisers can also hamper the process. For example, follow-up information beyond that supplied in the Information Memorandum may not be readily available, or they may have imposed an unrealistic timetable on the sale. Poorly-briefed sellers can lose their cool over run-of-the-mill terms with which they are unfamiliar. Preparation must, therefore, include agreeing your process with the other side.

Develop the integration plan in advance

A recurring theme throughout this book is that an acquirer cannot afford to arrive in the car park of its new business and start planning integration on the way to reception. This cannot be repeated often enough: if a buyer has not worked out what the synergy benefits are and how to obtain them well before taking control, it should not be doing the deal at all. Integration planning is a central part of the valuation. Valuation requires a clear view of the profit stream and, to state the obvious, this depends on the cost base and the sales line. The acquirer needs to be clear about any changes it will make to the cost base and the impact of its influence on sales and margins. When acquisitions go wrong, it often turns out that in the heat of trying to get the deal done, integration was left till the last minute, or even ignored. For example, in 1994, a cash-hungry BAe sold Rover to BMW for £800 m after problems with its regional jet business. BMW acquired Rover because it was struggling to develop its own off-road four-wheel drive vehicle and was attracted by the strong Land Rover brand. Unfortunately it also acquired Rover's cars business, for which BMW had no clear integration plan. It never managed to get to grips with Rover's Longbridge 'volume' car business and eventually sold it in 2000 to a management team at an estimated loss of €4.1 bn.

Integration management

The deal is done. The acquisition team is in the car park. Employees are casting sideways glances and talking with hushed voices. What happens next? The acquisition has to deliver the results which have been set out in spreadsheets, board papers and plans. Never mind all that sexy pre-deal strategy and negotiation stuff and all the outpourings of those clever advisers during due diligence, poor integration is the biggest reason for acquisition failure. This is where the real work begins.

Communicate ten times more often that you think is necessary

Acquirers need a pre-prepared communication plan which reflects the objectives of the deal and the circumstances of the acquired business. There is nothing like a takeover to generate stress, insecurity and ill-founded rumours, messages are all too easily misinterpreted and rumours spread. For example, a department meeting is called in the canteen. There are 30 chairs but 45 people, allowing some to leap to the conclusion that there will be 15 redundancies. Clear, rapid and consistent communication is essential. The sellers may be happy, but management, staff, customers, suppliers and other stakeholders did not ask for this change and they are all expecting the worst.

Not only do key messages have to be repeated over and over, but also they need to be reinforced by concrete actions. When communicating just after an acquisition, two of the golden rules are no hype and no empty promises.

Establish clear leadership from the beginning

Acquisition integration requires clear, strong leadership. There should be a single boss. This way there is a single point of reference, a single point of responsibility and a single point of decision making. Corus, the merger between British Steel and Hoogovens was never a great success because there were two bosses. Similarly, the Travellers/Citicorp integration was a disaster as the two leaders set about job-sharing. Worse, the next level of top jobs in the organisation were similarly shared. Jobs should be allocated on the basis of merit and ability; this is not the time for patronage and consensus.

Make changes quickly

Two other golden rules of acquisition integration are do it big and do it quick. Speed and decisiveness are critical. Change is expected and uncertainty builds until it is made. There will be tough decisions and there will be mistakes, but it is better to get the essential changes implemented than it is to dither and fuel uncertainty. HP and Compaq got this right: the top 1,500 job postings were announced on day one of the acquisition.

Recognise the scale of the task

As the integration process unfolds, the acquirer rarely finds that he has over-estimated the scale of the task. It takes experienced, senior resource, a detailed plan and contingencies for those larger than expected costs or drains on management. Credit Agricole only reaped half of the €574 m in initial savings it once expected from the first year of its merger with Crédit Lyonnais. Ford and BMW faced larger-than-expected integration tasks on acquiring Jaguar and Rover. Ten years after Marks and Spencer acquired Brooks Brothers a press campaign was finally launched trumpeting the success of the acquisition. Acquisition integration rarely proceeds more smoothly than originally anticipated. Research by AMR International[3] shows that the ideal target size is 5–10 per cent of the acquirer because at this size, the acquirer should have sufficient resources to manage integration.

Corporate development

After the excitement of the chase, the immediate satisfaction of the purchase and the first 100 days to establish control, comes the detailed and often tedious work needed to realise the benefits of the acquisition. The two businesses must be welded into one new organisation with a common direction and a common understanding. This can easily take up to three years to achieve.

Ensure changes are appropriate

Set against the needs for clarity of leadership and communication, and for rapid and effective action, comes the question of whether the acquirer has really understood whether its proposed changes will actually enhance the business. A 'one size fits all' or 'there is no alternative' approach to acquisition can spell disaster. For example, BAT failed to manage its non-tobacco subsidiaries effectively and exited from them. Equally the UK utilities all dabbled in the acquisition of non-regulated businesses after privatisation and mostly found that they were unable to achieve change which added value.

Do not ignore cultural differences

Effective integration requires people to work together. When cultures clash or the acquirer embarks on 'winner's syndrome', problems follow. Companies in the same market can have very different cultures. Look at British Airways and Virgin – and then add Ryanair to the mix. In this example cultural differences have grown out of different business models. National differences are also a rich source of cultural divergence.

One of the persisting problems with acquisitions is that they are still the province of lawyers and accountants. Lawyers and accountants deal with hard issues like contracts and balance sheets but getting the soft issues right – culture and management – will give the biggest chances of successful integration and therefore the biggest chance of a successful acquisition.

Acquirers need to understand cultures and manage accordingly. Two businesses with hugely divergent cultures cannot just be slammed together. For example, Sony and Matsushita have never come to grips with the freewheeling managers of the Californian film studios they acquired in the early 1990s.

Do not ignore customers

Customers pay the bills but are all too often relegated to second place as acquirers fall into the trap of focusing on internal reorganisation. They forget that customers do not necessarily leap for joy when they hear their supplier has been taken over. Equally they are not waiting for the acquirer to come and explain that its additional wonder product is the answer to their needs. Instead their thoughts turn to price rises, or worse. Then, just at that point, the representative of a rival firm makes an appointment to see them.

Almost every pharmaceutical merger in the 1990s resulted in a reduced market share for the combined businesses. Marks & Spencer considered it could do no wrong, but found that ignoring customers after the Littlewoods acquisition was a contributor to declining sales and market share.

The acquirer must put customers at the heart of an acquisition. The integration plan therefore needs to cater for customers in detail. This means worrying about how they will be served and who will communicate with them. Even if they will continue to be served in the same way, customers may well be sceptical about any benefits which the change in ownership will bring them. If their point of contact changes, or if their terms and conditions are altered, they will immediately be on their guard and more open to the approaches of alternative suppliers.

Do not ignore the core

When acquiring, the focus of management attention naturally turns to the acquired business. Whilst all this is going on, the core business is expected to perform as usual. This can only happen if the acquirer has prepared a clear plan for how it will run its own business while it diverts resources to buying and integrating other businesses.

Airfix, the once dominant UK plastic model kit maker, destroyed its highly profitable core business by focusing entirely on acquisition. The management left behind to run the core business was strongly production focused and failed to innovate. Competitors met the needs of dissatisfied customers and stole its markets. Managers who go off and spend time in other – more exciting – areas need to ensure that their jobs in the core business are still carried out.

Conclusion

Acquisitions are risky; they can fail for a wide range of reasons. In reality it is a combination of mistakes which lead to most failures. Success requires the firm foundations of the right strategy, a willingness to get into the detail, sound execution of the deal and then in the integration phase a prepared plan decisively followed through. All this means preparing and taking the right advice, planning and making the right resource available and then coupling this with strong management and clear direction.

The upside of successful acquisitions is substantial. They can make money in their own right; they can also bring commercial or tactical advantage to the enlarged acquirer. The proof lies in the highest rated companies. Very few of the world's top businesses have achieved success without acquisition. But acquisitions are just one strategic development tool along with joint ventures, licence or distribution agreements, organic growth and disposals.

Notes

1 For example, McKinsey (Quarterly 2001 Number 4) seems to point to sales being lost in acquisitions and, according to the Financial Times, 'Most mergers that fail do so because revenue growth stalls during integration and fails to recover' (*Financial Times*, May 6th 2002).

2 See page 114.

3 AMR acquisition knowledge base; Rankine, D., *Why Acquisitions Fail*, Financial Times Prentice Hall, 2001.

Finding candidates **2**

Introduction: have a sound acquisition plan

The most successful acquisitions are those that fit within a predetermined strategic plan but as the ideal targets are rarely immediately for sale, acquirers may have to react opportunistically when the right target companies become available. Well-run groups keep a watching brief on good acquisition candidates. Their homework allows them to react when a business becomes available. It also avoids the difficulty of having to convince a sceptical board of the logic of a previously unadvertised deal.

Figure 2.1 below shows that purely opportunistic acquisitions have the lowest success rate. Those acquisitions which were identified opportunistically, but which were part of a predetermined strategy and those acquisitions that resulted from a structured search were more successful.

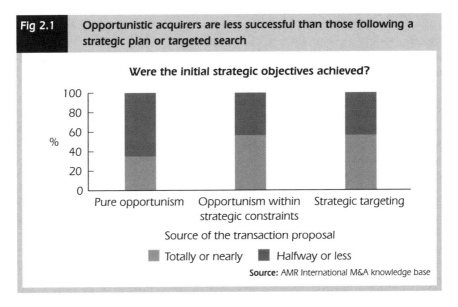

Fig 2.1 Opportunistic acquirers are less successful than those following a strategic plan or targeted search

Were the initial strategic objectives achieved?

Source of the transaction proposal

■ Totally or nearly   ■ Halfway or less

Source: AMR International M&A knowledge base

Before setting its acquisition criteria and embarking on deals, the acquirer should already know why it is acquiring. This includes understanding what a particular acquisition will bring in terms of market access or core competences and how it will be run alongside existing businesses.

Buying a business simply because it is available is not a good idea. For example, Benson plc, a small British specialist engineering group, had been turned around and it successfully bolted on two small acquisitions to its core business. It then acquired another business in a non-core area, rubber mouldings. The logic for the acquisition was that the last time it acquired from this particular seller the deal turned out to be a bargain. This acquisition did not add value to the group, it became a major diversion when performance dipped further and it dragged the whole group into receivership.

Acquisition criteria

Acquisition criteria are derived from the strategic reasons for acquisition. They need not be complicated, in fact the more precise they are the better. Think of it like buying a house. If you tell an estate agent you want to buy 15 Acacia Avenue he or she knows exactly what to do next. If you say you want a three-bedroom semi somewhere in the south east of England the agents will come back with such a long list of potential properties you will not know where to start. One acquisition search for facilities management companies yielded eight hundred names and got nowhere whereas an engineering company that worked out where it could add value to an acquisition specified a tight list of criteria which led to a short-list of three candidates and then to a deal.

Acquisition criteria comprise a mix of 'hard' and 'soft' issues. 'Hard' issues are quantifiable, such as revenues or employee numbers; 'soft' include skills or culture. It is often powerful to specifically exclude aspects of a target, or elements of its business model, which are unsuitable. For example, no unprofitable businesses, or no contract publishers, or no companies with more than 10 per cent sales to the automotive industry.

Table 2.1 sets out some example acquisition criteria, split between hard and soft issues.

Target identification methods

Having defined what it is looking for, an acquirer must now identify the right acquisition candidates. Large groups with a strong acquisition track record tend to attract opportunities, but even with this natural 'deal flow' they do not always identify or attract all of the opportunities that are relevant to them. Smaller businesses and those that are less visible as potential acquirers can find it even harder to attract opportunities, often not being offered the opportunity to bid for businesses which would make a good fit simply because they are 'not on the radar' as an acquirer.

Table 2.1	Example acquisition criteria

Acquisition criteria should relate to strategy; they should be simple and look further than financials

Example acquisition criteria

Hard/financial	Soft/operational
• Size	• Skill sets
– Turnover, employees	– People, accreditations
• Business area	• Customer groups
– Products, services	– Key customers, industry segments
• Geography	• Operations
– Markets served, distribution	– Actual activities, sales spilts
• Facilities	• Sources of incremental value
– Locations	– Contracts, skills, relationships
Published information	*Unpublished information*

Acquirers can attract or identify opportunities in a number of ways. These are:

- Exploiting contacts and knowledge within the business
- Communicating an acquisition profile to introducers
- Building a database of targets through research
- Advertising
- Waiting to be approached by potential sellers

No single one of these methods is the best. They can all work, which is why successful acquirers use a combination of them.

Exploiting contacts and knowledge within the business

Should the prospective acquirer's strategy call for an acquisition of a close competitor, a supplier or even a customer, there will already be a great deal of knowledge to tap within the acquirer's own business. Operational management are aware of the players within their sector and they may already know the management and some of the shareholders. They will also be very well placed to provide insights into their strengths, weaknesses and potential fit with the acquirer. All this makes it very straightforward for the acquirer's operational managers to develop a profile of some prospective targets.

However, you should also remember that this resource has inbuilt bias. Line managers see the weaknesses in rivals and they can hold strong views born of the scars of battle. Their knowledge may also be out-of-date, particularly of more distant businesses which they come across rarely. Finally, their opinions will be more operational than strategic – there is nothing which excites a sales director more than buying out the competition.

Acquisitive groups are usually good at finding ways to meet the shareholders of businesses they are interested in. They are able to explore avenues of potential cooperation. A major benefit of using internal knowledge is that, where relationships exist at the right level, it may be relatively easy to find the environment in which to open discussions with the owners. The ideal is then to form a relationship with the business and its owners. This will be on both a business and a personal level. If the personal relationship works it is all the easier to sell the benefits of fit between the businesses. Of course, if the strategy is right and the target is right, both sides should see the benefits. Figure 2.2 below sets out the simple virtuous circle of the 'sweetheart deal'. At the very least, an introductory meeting can be used to leave a marker, making it clear that you would be interested in a discussion should the shareholders decide to sell. Should the business be put up for sale, the shareholders will inform their corporate finance advisers of any such approaches and these will undoubtedly be followed up.

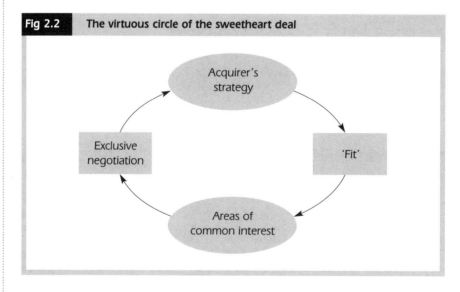

Fig 2.2 — The virtuous circle of the sweetheart deal

Communicating an acquisition profile to introducers

Acquirers who want to ensure that they see as many relevant deals as possible stay in touch with the 'introducers'. These introducers range from investment banks through the large, medium and, sometimes, small accounting firms, with corporate finance activities to corporate finance boutiques to wealth managers and individual brokers or consultants. Introducers can either be generalists working on a wide range of deals, or sector specialists.

You need to keep in touch with the introducers in whom you have confidence. Keeping them up to date with your acquisition criteria keeps your name in front of them and helps you get onto their call lists when they are looking for buyers. Good intermediaries will be selective in who they invite to look at a business.

Staying in touch also has the advantage of sparking possible ideas for the acquisition of a business that is not officially for sale. For example when discussing an acquisition brief and the reasons for fit, an introducer may be able to make a suggestion based on his knowledge of the sector and of the intentions of the companies he or she deals with. Introducers can then start the process of brokering a deal, starting on a 'no-names' basis if need be.

Prospective acquirers should make sure they look like a good option when presenting themselves to introducers. Personal relationships can count for a lot but introducers will also be asking other questions. Most of them will work on a contingent basis (i.e. they only get paid when a deal completes) which means that their main concerns will revolve around your ability to complete a transaction. They will ask themselves questions such as:

- Is it realistic about financing acquisitions?
- Does this acquirer have a serious strategy?
- Has it got board approval to acquire?
- Has it got the procedures and resources to complete the transaction?
- Will it be prepared to pay my introduction fee (should there be one)?

Auctions

The downside of dealing with introducers is that you end up on the long list of companies which are invited into a controlled auction. In a seller's market this means being given a glossy but rather vague information memorandum, which is often known as a 'black book' and being asked to name a price. Access to management, further information and the company's facilities ranges from non-existent through stage-managed to reasonable.

These auctions are not for the faint-hearted. By definition the successful bidder will have overpaid. You should only enter an auction if you have the inside track and that means having done a lot of homework.

Building a database of targets through research

Serious acquirers build a database of targets as a part of their acquisition screening and monitoring process. This approach is particularly appropriate in fragmented markets or unknown territories, where the acquirer lacks the advantage of in-house contacts or a reputation as a serious acquirer amongst local introducers. It is also the only way of doing a sweetheart deal and thereby avoiding auctions. A systematic approach, designed to search out the most appropriate opportunities, can go a long way to preventing the disappointment of finding that a suitable acquisition was missed. This information can also form the start point for the evaluation process once negotiations start with a target.

Some acquirers even use their database as a negotiating tool, by leaving their target company's owners in little doubt that the acquirer has a number of choices and is, therefore, unlikely to overpay. Exasperated by the antics of its US counterpart, one chairman of a UK plc thumped a thick acquisition search report on the table and shouted, 'I have a lot more companies to go and negotiate with if we don't get this deal sorted out soon'. The transaction completed a matter of days later.

The objectives of a systematic search are to find out:

• What companies are in the market?
• How close is their fit to the acquirer's acquisition criteria?
• Who owns them (independent shareholders, managers, parent companies)?
• Whether they are available?

An advantage of a search is that it allows you to select acquisition targets based on their quality of fit, as opposed to availability. In other words it does not just consider the one or two companies put forward by introducers, but assesses the whole range of businesses with a good fit to the acquisition strategy and acquisition criteria. With a coherent basic knowledge of each target and its competitors, the prospective acquirer has at least the basis for making a decision, determining which ones to approach and possibly proceeding into initial discussions. Of course you will need a lot more detail on the target if you decide to go on and make an offer for the business.

The effort required to research a market for a list of acquisition candidates will depend greatly on the characteristics of the desired acquisition. For instance, if the search is limited to a narrow market or businesses with a large turnover in a single country then the numbers involved will be limited.

The researchers building the database can call on the plethora of available information sources. These include:

- Financial and company databases
- General trade directories (e.g. Kompass, Kelly's etc)
- Trade associations
- Industry periodicals and directories (as listed in Benn's Media Guide)
- Trade show directories/catalogues
- Buyer's guides
- Financial surveys (e.g. Jordan's, Keynote etc)
- Published market reports (e.g. Mintel, Euromonitor etc)
- In-house knowledge
- Suppliers and customers of the industry

If no acquisition results from a search it means that no appropriate company is available. The sector can then be monitored for developments and in the meantime resources can be more usefully directed elsewhere. For example, the European industrial ceramics business went through a period of consolidation in the 1980s and 1990s as many companies were acquired, leaving a handful of significant companies in independent ownership. Prospective acquirers, having established contact with each of the remaining companies could take no further action in the sector and had to concentrate development resources elsewhere.

Should an opportunity to acquire arise at a later stage within the screened sector the acquirer will have an understanding of all the potential targets and will be able rapidly to compare the available company with its competitors.

The acquirer's staff may have sufficient resources, industry knowledge and contacts for this process to be conducted in-house. If this is not the case, it may make sense to use search consultants. Their role is discussed in more detail later in this chapter.

Advertising

Apart from smaller deals in certain sectors, advertising is not a particularly effective way of finding opportunities. The exception is in those industries, such as retail and hotels, where businesses are regularly advertised for sale in the trade press. Acquirers can scour these advertisements and bid for those of interest. Outside the specific trade press in these industries, an acquirer will typically find searching advertisements a frustrating experience. They encounter the frustration that some of the sellers who advertise are not entirely serious about the sale of the business, or are not particularly well-organised. Businesses for sale that are not advised by a corporate finance house tend to be the least serious.

Only the most undiscerning and opportunistic acquirers should advertise for candidates to acquire. They will find that the enquiries they attract are not particularly serious or attractive.

Waiting to be approached by sellers

Alternatively companies can wait to be approached by sellers. Whilst this may work reasonably well for well-known companies, even experienced acquirers do not rely entirely on opportunities coming to them. Less-well-known buyers will have to be very patient if all they do is sit and wait for the ideal opportunity to come along.

Using outside help

External organisations can play an important role as catalysts in the acquisition process. The role of intermediaries as mandated sellers of businesses and as brokers of ideas has been mentioned above. Acquirers can also retain external organisations to perform a structured search or help understand target companies. The occasions when this makes the most sense are when:

• Targets are sought in a fragmented or opaque market
• Targets are sought in unknown territories
• The acquirer requires insight into a seemingly attractive target about which it has insufficient knowledge

Running an acquisition search

The use of consultants requires a clear research brief, a statement of the work to be carried out by both sides and a specification of the outputs required. Otherwise, especially in fragmented or difficult sectors, you run the risk of results not coming up to expectations with at best the M&A equivalent of a list of three-bedroom houses in the south east of England. Consultants can be used for a single exercise, or they can be briefed to monitor a sector for the availability of companies through changing circumstances.

A single review of a sector for targets is best conducted when time is of the essence; a framework is required for comparing one or two targets which have already been identified, or to confirm that no unknown opportunities exist and therefore that resources are best redirected elsewhere. Table 2.2 below sets out the typical acquisition search process.

Table 2.2	Typical acquisition search process			
Phase	*Acquirer's role*	*Searcher's role*	*Result*	*No. of companies*
Strategy	Develop and refine strategy	Understand acquirer's strategy. Translate it into clear acquisition criteria	Well-defined acquisition criteria	Unknown
Identify universe of acquisition candidates	Share in-house information including known candidates and sources	Use the best information sources. Identify all businesses meeting the criteria	Database of all possible candidates	100–800
Screening	Provide feedback on progress	Investigate every company using phone research and desk research	Snapshot of each candidate containing key data relating to acquisition criteria	80–200
Shortlist review	Review fit between candidates and acquisition strategy	Provide strategic insights and advice	Prioritised shortlist of top candidates	3–30
Evaluation	Use industry knowledge to refine shortlist	Further desk research or meetings on no-names basis with key managers/ shareholders	Clear view of which candidates should be approached and how	3–12
Approach	Decide method of approach and key messages	Advice on approach methodology and assistance where required	Companies to negotiate with	3–6
Negotiation	Embark on negotiations	Support based on knowledge	Heads of agreement	1–3
Due diligence	Orchestration of process	Support based on knowledge	Successful acquisition	One at a time!

A rolling approach to screening and monitoring a sector is best used in an industry with a large number of participants where a series of transactions is proposed.

Search consultants are often prepared to take a significant proportion of their fee on success, although they will invariably require a fixed fee element for their work. Those who accept the highest proportion of contingent fee will be more deal-driven and perhaps less discerning; those preferring to avoid highly contingent fees tend to be more strategic. The selection of consultants will revolve around trust and a view of their ability to perform. It is worth ensuring that they will use original industry research and that the project will not be entirely staffed by juniors.

The following case study sets out the example of an acquisition search conducted by a search consultancy on behalf of a group, which had taken the strategic decision to increase its share of the liquid waste business. Due to the impending consolidation of the UK industry time was of the essence and targets were sought in a highly fragmented market.

Case study 2.1 UK waste management acquisition search

Acquirer

Water utility, with a limited operation in liquid waste transport, treatment and disposal

Objective

1 Review market structure, growth prospects, entry barriers and opportunities in each selected geographic region.
2 Identify acquisition targets.

Parameters

Targets were sought which fell within the following parameters:

- Involved in the transport of liquid industrial waste
- Involved in the treatment of liquid industrial waste
- Profitable, or at least breaking even
- Preferably owner-managed
- Ownership of, or guaranteed access to, licensed disposal sites
- Minimum size: five owned tankers
- Manufacturing customer base preferred
- Industrial cleaning excluded

▶

Method

1 All relevant companies were identified using industrial and local directories, contact with major customers and regulators.

2 A database of 400 potential targets was developed.

3 Each one of the potential targets was contacted to ascertain whether they matched the acquisition parameters.

4 Those companies which failed to meet basic size, capability and service criteria were eliminated.

5 A first shortlist was reviewed with the acquirer, and targets were prioritised. The top 15 companies were selected.

6 Face-to-face interviews were arranged with the shareholders and senior management (they were often the same) of the 15 companies with the best fit. These meetings resulted in detailed profiles on each one as an acquisition target. Information already obtained was confirmed and significant further detail was added about each operation. The market position of each company was confirmed and the aspirations of shareholders, including their willingness to join forces with a major company, were investigated. The acquirer's anonymity was retained during this phase.

7 The results were reviewed by the acquirer. Three companies were rejected as unsuitable acquisition targets. (One of them was treating five times more waste than the capacity of its facility, which was situated over a disused mineshaft!)

8 Introductions were made to the owners of 12 of the targeted companies. The manner of each introduction was tailored to the shareholders' circumstances and aspirations.

Result

On the basis of the information obtained and the relationships created with the 12 companies introduced to the acquiring group, eight targets chose to enter into discussions, and two were acquired. This result was achieved in a competitive market with a number of other players simultaneously seeking to consolidate the sector.

The water company continued to grow the business through organic means. Meanwhile, the database of potential targets allowed new opportunities to be evaluated as they arose over the following years as industry consolidation continued.

Obtaining more than a basic profile on the business

As in the case study, some acquirers choose to invite their consultants to go on and run the initial evaluation stage. The consultants have an advantage as they can seek and obtain information using professional interviewing skills from managers who might otherwise be reluctant to speak to an acquirer directly. The use of face-to-face interviews alongside telephone interviews and desk research gives the best available results. They can also approach shareholders so as to understand their intentions on a 'no-names' basis.

On other occasions acquirers ask market or strategic consultants to conduct a 'pre-exclusivity' due diligence study of a target. This is a very powerful tool, but can only be justified when the acquirer has good reason to believe that a transaction is possible.

In any event once an acquirer has a number of candidates in its sights it can monitor them, gathering information and insights from a range of sources and contracts. All this information helps to form a better view of the business and allows the acquirer to be better prepared should it have the opportunity to negotiate with any of the companies.

Timing

For many acquirers timing is as big a problem as finding the targets. Acquirers may have hired expensive strategy consultants to define their future direction and have a shortlist of businesses in their sights, but none is available. Indeed, if the shortlist comprises only one or two decent targets, the acquirer may have to worry about its overall acquisition and growth strategy.

When availability is difficult acquirers can increase their chances of success by attempting to form a relationship with the target companies. The objective is to be called first when the target does become available. If the two businesses have a strong and coherent fit the idea of working together can start to take shape. This approach is often difficult for competitors to put into practice, but it could be achieved, for example, through a joint venture to enter a new market or territory together. It could be a joint supply arrangement to obtain better rates from suppliers, or an industry benchmarking club. Obviously this route has significant advantages as the two businesses become natural partners, also the management teams get to know each other and it becomes clear how well they can work together. The evaluation will in fact have begun.

Conclusion

Experienced acquirers often comment that finding the company to acquire is the easy part of the exercise. The secret is to start with a well-worked-out business development strategy. This will help in drawing up a focused list of acquisition criteria which can be communicated to third parties and used to look for and screen potential targets.

Identifying targets is one thing, but there is no guarantee that they will be available. Monitoring targets for their availability should therefore be seen as a continuing activity as indeed should be the policy of keeping intermediaries warm.

Preliminary negotiations 3

There is usually a long run into an acquisition during which the two sides make some 'preliminary agreements'. Most will be agreements on how the parties will behave during the negotiations but some will make it into the final sale and purchase agreement. Most will not be binding, but some will be. You do not want to find yourself unwittingly bound by a preliminary agreement which you had assumed was not binding; this is why you should involve your lawyers although they can often make what might seem like an unnecessary fuss.

The most common pre-contractual documents are the confidentiality agreement and the letter of intent and it is these that we will examine in this chapter.

The confidentiality agreement

The pre-acquisition period is a lot like the dance of the seven veils. The prospective target will slowly reveal more and more so that the buyer can decide whether or not to go ahead. The prospective target is very vulnerable because it will be revealing more and more confidential information with no guarantee that the deal will complete. Therefore, despite a general obligation to negotiate in good faith, the seller will want an informal confidentiality agreement in which both sides agree their rights and obligations.

The things you will need to think about and agree are set out below.

Who signs?

This should be the easy bit. Usually, but not always, there are only two parties – you and the seller. The point is that if you and the seller are companies, the entire company is bound. The confidentiality agreement sometimes mentions who within each company is authorised to receive and to give the information. Naming individuals like this is designed to organise the exchange of information from company to company. In addition agreements nearly always have a clause binding advisers, which is what you want because it means you can pass on information received without separate negotiations. All they have to do is agree to be bound by the same agreement as you.

What is covered?

You may need to think carefully about what information is covered. The other side will want to draft this part as broadly as possible but if, for example, you are in the same industry as the target, a lot of what lawyers think is confidential information you may already have. Because no-one can be expected to keep information confidential if it is not confidential in the first place, confidentiality agreements usually contain a list of things which are not covered:

- Information which is, or comes into, the public domain through no act of the receiving party which is in breach of the agreement
- Information which was already in the possession of the receiving party
- Information which is independently developed by the receiving party
- Information which is received from another source without any restriction on use or disclosure

If you are given confidential information which the authorities order you to disclose you would not be in breach of a confidentiality agreement. To cater for this somewhat unlikely event confidentiality agreements stipulate that if a party receives such a disclosure order, it should immediately tell the other side so that it can take appropriate action.

How long does it last?

There has to be a time limit on a secrecy obligation. You cannot be expected to keep silent forever – it would be like having the sword of Damocles hanging over you. Besides information loses its value pretty quickly. The norm is usually between three and five years.

If the non-disclosure obligation is for an undetermined period or just not mentioned in the agreement, which is not unusual, its actual duration will be decided by the relevant law. In some jurisdictions, for example under French law, any party may terminate an agreement with no time limit by sending the other party a termination notice. This is quite dangerous because that party could then communicate the privileged information to third parties. For this reason it is advisable to have a time limit in the confidentiality agreement.

What happens if it is breached?

Confidentiality agreements, unlike some letters of intent, contain contractually binding obligations. Violation of these obligations is a breach of contract giving the other side the right to sue for full compensation for the damage suffered. Damage would be determined by the courts or may have been set out in a penalty clause in the agreement.

In practice, it is also very difficult to prove even that a secrecy obligation has been violated and proving that you have suffered loss is also very difficult. Both factors may explain why there are so few court cases for breaches of confidentiality agreements. But this does not stop lawyers from taking them extremely seriously. Confidentiality agreements can go back and forth between legal advisers several times, racking up their fees. Principals need to be aware of this and decide how much value is actually being added.

The letter of intent

The letter of intent is another preliminary agreement. It is referred to under a variety of names, including 'memorandum of understanding', 'commitment letter', 'binder', 'agreement in principle', 'Heads of Agreement', 'Heads of Terms' or 'Heads'.

Heads of Terms is a written document generally exchanged between the parties when negotiations have reached an advanced stage, usually at the point where there is agreement to agree. At this point both sides usually want to formalise their intentions and expectations before proceeding. Its function is to summarise the broad terms of what has been agreed and put in writing how the negotiations are expected to continue before both sides embark on the detail of finishing off the transaction. The parties do not normally want Heads to be binding because they do not want to be on the hook until negotiations have reached a satisfactory conclusion. Nonetheless, they do want reasonable assurance that they are not about to waste a great deal of time and money trying to get the deal done. That is the function of the letter of intent. While it may not be binding it does at least force both parties to take stock of where they are and what they want to happen from here.

Negotiating Heads is therefore very important to the final outcome of the deal and it is worth thinking about the agenda in some detail. From an acquirer's perspective the following list covers the main issues, but the order of events must be down to judgement on the day. Topics will include some or all of the following:

1 **Update since last meeting.** It is vital to clarify even at this late stage any change of information which affects the deal.
2 **Confirmation of what is included.** It is possible that misunderstandings still exist – what are the key assets to be included in the deal?

3 **Price of certain assets to be purchased by directors.** This is a sensitive but necessary part of the negotiation process, and must form part of the acquisition price.

4 **Timetable.** This is a good opportunity to agree the timetable and as a by-product secure all access and cooperation you need for due diligence. Both sides will want to move as quickly as possible but of the two, sellers will be the keenest. Make sure you get enough time to do everything you want. Allow six weeks for due diligence to give enough time for briefing advisers and, more importantly, digesting their findings. You may need two weeks or more on top of that to negotiate the agreement, carry out any pre-completion stock-takes and so on.

5 **Obligations of the parties during negotiations.** For example the buyer will want access to management and customers to carry out due diligence.

6 **Earn-out formula and period.** All too often earn-out deals are not clarified in sufficient detail. It is important to illustrate the earn-out formula with examples to ensure all parties understand the deal.

7 **Transfer of pension funds.** The complexity of pensions is frequently underestimated. Sufficient time is required to resolve the issues. It is quite acceptable for the detailed administration of pension funds to be transferred and finalised over a 6–12 month period post completion.

8 **Intellectual property rights.** When intellectual property is a major reason for the deal, buyers must ensure that the relevant rights are owned by the target company and that they do not rest with individual directors, contractors or other companies outside the target.

9 **Removal of personal guarantees.** In private companies especially, directors may be standing behind loans or other liabilities. Buyers will have to offer the release of guarantees.

10 **Key warranties and indemnities.** These are discussed in detail in Chapter 8 (The sale and purchase agreement). At this stage it is important to flag the main warranties and indemnities expected.

11 **Purchase price and consideration.** The final price negotiations must be agreed at this meeting and its position on the agenda should be driven by the acquirer.

12 **Standstill agreement or 'exclusivity'.** Another very important concern for buyers is that the seller might hold parallel negotiations with third parties. A standstill agreement is an agreement in which the seller agrees not to conduct negotiations with third parties for a limited time to give the buyer a clear run at getting the deal done. Heads of Terms signal that there is an

agreement to agree. From the point they are signed, the buyer will start spending time and money to complete the transaction. There is no point in a buyer going to all the time, trouble and expense involved in completing an acquisition if it is not reasonably confident of a positive outcome. While this can never be guaranteed there is clearly a much lower chance of success if another party is still in the running. The existence of parallel negotiations can also adversely affect the buyer's bargaining position. Its negotiating strategy would be very different if it knew that in effect it was in an auction. From a strictly legal point of view, there is no need for the seller to disclose parallel negotiations hence the frequent use of standstill agreements and as a buyer you should always demand a period of exclusivity.

13 **Secret research and development.** Where the acquirer and the target company are competitors in an industry which requires continuing secret research and development, an abortive transaction may lead to allegations from the seller that the acquirer has used the potential transaction as a ruse to gain access to the target company's ideas. The acquirer may be required to enter a specific agreement to cover this possibility and to establish an agreed dispute resolution procedure.

14 **Binding provisions.** Various binding provisions can be negotiated into Heads of Terms. These are covered later in this chapter.

A letter of intent gives comfort to both parties that the other side is serious. However, practitioners in the mergers and acquisitions arena disagree widely about the desirability and enforceability of letters of intent, which is what we will now look at.

Advantages of a letter of intent

There are three definite advantages of a letter of intent.

It speeds up the deal and makes final agreement easier

The fact that the parties agree on the basic terms and structure of a proposed transaction gives them comfort that they will be able to agree in the future on the detailed points which will inevitably crop up later. The letter of intent generally serves as a good roadmap for the final agreement. It may also be used to guide the negotiation process itself.

It can contain binding provisions which help get the deal done

A letter of intent may not itself be binding but it usually contains some binding provisions which are important in getting to agreement. While they could be agreed separately, with a letter of intent you have them all under one roof and, more importantly, you only need one set of negotiations. These are generally:

- *The confidentiality clause.* The confidentiality clause binds both buyer and seller not to disclose to a third party any information discovered in the course of the transaction, the terms of the proposed transaction or even the existence of the letter of intent itself. This provision may also have been included in the confidentiality agreement (covered above)

- *The standstill clause.* As already mentioned, the standstill clause is the provision by which the parties agree that the seller will not negotiate or deal with a third party while the buyer and seller are negotiating a definitive agreement

- *A 'no-solicitation' provision.* To reinforce the standstill clause, the letter of intent may also contain a 'no-solicitation' provision which forbids the seller from soliciting, encouraging, entering into discussions or providing information to any third party bidder

- *Give-and-take issues.* In the letter of intent the parties may clearly set out the conditions that need to be settled before the transaction can be finalised. If one of these conditions is not met both sides are in no doubt as to where they stand

- *Expenses and fees.* A letter of intent may also include a provision saying who will pay which fees and other costs if the transaction is not consummated. Usually, each party bears its own expenses unless one of the parties abruptly or unlawfully terminates negotiations. In this case, a penalty, known as a 'break fee', may kick in. This is established in the agreement to compensate the other party

- *Indemnification against liabilities.* It is also advisable to include in a letter of intent a clause establishing that one party will indemnify the other against any potential liabilities which may arise because of the proposed transaction

- *Defensive clause.* The letter of intent may also include some defensive provisions, such as 'lock-up' or termination fees, designed to compensate the buyer if the proposed transaction is not consummated due to a third party bidder

It can help with financing

Finally, the letter of intent may be useful to the buyer who needs to raise finance. Banks and other lenders often want to see a letter of intent before committing to financing a transaction.

Disadvantages of a letter of intent

The three most discussed disadvantages of the letter of intent are the following.

It might be difficult to renegotiate

Once the parties have set out the key transaction points, such as price, the letter of intent may make it difficult for either party subsequently to negotiate on such points.

Any price mentioned in a letter of intent will be an estimate because the parties have not started due diligence. The price mentioned in the letter of intent, therefore, should be stated as subject to due diligence.

Negotiating a letter of intent may delay the transaction

Negotiating a letter of intent may create an unnecessary delay in signing the final agreement. Especially when time is short, it is sometimes preferable to proceed directly to the definitive agreement.

Additionally, the attempt to achieve too much in the letter of intent may be fruitless before the parties have conducted their due diligence.

It can lead to unintended obligations

Depending on the wording of the letter of intent, both the buyer and the seller risk being unwittingly bound by provisions that they intended as non-binding.

Enforceability of the letter of intent

A major concern when drafting a letter of intent should be its enforceability. In general, the seller wants it to be as binding as possible, the buyer, on the other hand, usually wants the opposite.

There is always a debate as to whether a letter of intent is a binding and enforceable contract or whether it is an unenforceable agreement to agree. The answer is: it depends on which jurisdiction you are in. Anglo-Saxon M&A practitioners will tell you that Heads of Terms are non-binding 'agreements to agree' unless the parties specifically provide otherwise. In Napoleonic jurisdictions it is possible for the parties to be legally bound by Heads of Terms even if they do not want to be because European courts examine the intent of the parties and how definite the agreement is in order to determine its enforceability. They usually examine:

- The context of the negotiations
- The language used in the letter of intent
- Whether the subject matter of the negotiations concerns complicated matters that customarily require a definitive written agreement

- The parties' respective degrees of performance of the letter of intent's terms
- The size and complexity of outstanding issues which remain unresolved

Therefore, outside the Anglo-Saxon countries, if the parties wish to avoid being bound by their letter of intent, the language of the letter must clearly say so. Bear the following in mind:

- The text of the introductory paragraph should clearly state that the purpose of the letter is to create either a wholly non-binding or a combination of binding and non-binding obligations
- It may also be helpful to refer to the buyer as the 'Prospective Buyer' and the selling shareholders as 'Prospective Sellers' to emphasise the contingent nature of the transaction
- Where non-binding provisions are desired, use conditional language such as 'would' and 'might'. Conversely, where the parties wish to create a binding agreement, words such as 'shall' and 'will' must be used
- List everything that needs to be done before the definitive agreement can be signed
- In a concluding paragraph, state that the letter of intent is generally non-binding, but list the paragraphs by number that are intended to bind the parties. To reinforce this, binding and non-binding provisions should be in separate sections
- It is helpful to state that other than with the 'Binding Paragraphs', a signature on the letter of intent shall not be considered as evidence of intent of the Prospective Seller or Prospective Buyer to be bound by the terms of the letter
- If the parties want an entirely non-binding letter of intent the document should be short and, in order to avoid judicial misinterpretation of the intent, the parties should not sign such a letter
- Finally, it is worth noting that every deal is different and therefore that the specifics of the deal will dictate the way in which the letter of intent is drafted

Conclusion

This chapter has demystified the two most important documents exchanged in the lead up to final negotiations: the confidentiality agreement and the letter of intent. Both can be long and virtually impenetrable. Keeping the basics in mind is a great aid to understanding. For confidentiality agreements these are: who and what does it cover, how long does it last and what are the chances of being sued if it all goes wrong? For letters of intent the basic questions are: do I want one, and if so, what should go in it and how much of it do I want to be enforceable?

The integration plan  4

I t is no accident that this chapter comes where it does in this book. You must start thinking about integration the second you start getting serious about an acquisition. It is not something which should be left until the ink dries on the deal documentation. However well the strategy has been worked out and however well the deal has been transacted, no acquisition is ever going to be successful if there is no plan for the aftermath – or if that plan is not properly executed. This may sound perfectly obvious, but poor integration is the single biggest reason for acquisitions to fail and the reason integration is so poorly carried out is that it gets forgotten. One of the sad facts of life, still, is that corporate M&A departments work in isolation of the business. They interpret their brief as finding and transacting acquisitions. Most private equity houses are no different. Success and reward come from finding and transacting deals. Managing the portfolio is a backwater.

The golden rules of acquisition integration

There are four golden rules for acquisition integration:

- *Plan early*. Acquisition integration should begin before due diligence and continue through the pre-deal process
- *Minimise uncertainty* by moving quickly, communicating fully and getting early wins
- *Manage properly*. Integration management is a full-time job
- *Soft issues are paramount* and far more important than driving out the cost savings

We will consider each of these in turn before going on to look at the integration plan and its execution.

Plan early

There are three reasons for planning integration at the earliest stage possible:

- Without again wishing to state the obvious, if you have no clear idea of where and how you are going to find extra value it is impossible to value the business
- Post-deal integration is vital to success and one of the best ways of collecting the information needed for integration planning on the business and its markets is through due diligence. The alternative is waiting until the deal is

done but by then it is too late. There are strong arguments, therefore for starting integration planning before due diligence kicks off so that potential integration issues can be identified during due diligence, just as legal or accounting issues would be

- Two of the key drivers of post-acquisition success demand early planning. To increase the chances of success, acquirers should:
  - Make people-related integration changes as soon as possible after the deal. People decisions therefore need to be made early
  - Make integration as speedy as possible so that there are early victories which demonstrate progress. The need for speed means taking decisions based on information that is more incomplete than usual but the more the missing pieces of information can be collected before the integration phase starts, the quicker the integration can proceed

Let us look at these points in more detail.

The link between integration, valuation and due diligence

The cash flows of the combined businesses will depend on how the businesses are run. Integration planning therefore has a direct input to valuation and, as already mentioned, the due diligence phase should include critical testing and challenging of the estimated synergies. These are often misjudged. Figure 4.1 shows the relationship between integration, valuation and due diligence.

Post-acquisition planning should address the most important issues which impact on valuation; the most important of these are where synergy benefits are going to come from and how they are going to be realised. A deal has the best chances of success when it helps create competitive advantage and therefore profit growth. Due diligence questions which have impact on value include:

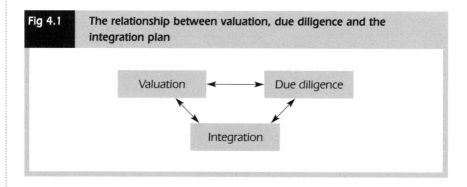

Fig 4.1   **The relationship between valuation, due diligence and the integration plan**

- Sources of post-deal competitive advantage
- Investment required to upgrade equipment and plant
- Systems changes and upgrades
- Property and facilities changes
- Personnel changes
- Changes to products, suppliers and customers

Private equity investors develop detailed business plans with their management teams, which are effectively integration plans, before a deal is completed. Acquirers should do the same. These plans should work from the same financial forecasts as are used for the valuation.

Since there must be a connection between the strategic thinking behind an acquisition and the approach to its integration, it should be a short hop and a skip from acquisition strategy to the creation of a structured framework within which the assets of the acquired company (people, plant, processes, intellectual property) can be combined with those of the acquirer to generate the highest possible levels of return. The starting point for integration, therefore, must be the rationale for the deal in the first place.

Acquisition rationale drives the plan

The main reasons for acquiring are shown in Table 4.1. As can be seen, there are only five.

Being crystal-clear on the acquisition rationale and on what the acquisition is supposed to achieve will help define the broad framework for integration. Use due diligence to help fill in the details, specifically to help:

- Define how closely the acquiring company can integrate the target company into its existing operations
- Identify major cultural, structural or legal factors which influence the speed and direction of integration
- Identify the operational demands of integration
- Provide a clear project plan for senior management, with associated tasks, resource requirements, timelines, and milestones

Table 4.1	The strategic reasons for an acquisition		
	Strategic objectives	*Integration objectives*	*Major issues*
To rationalise capacity in an industry	To increase prices and lower costs by eliminating industry capacity and gaining market power through increased share and increasing scale efficiencies	Speedy rationalisation	Systems and facilities integration. Customer retention
To consolidate a fragmented industry	To gain a cost advantage through creating economies of scale in the operations of localised operations	Rationalisation of systems, procedures and 'back offices'	Maintenance of customer service. Retention of key staff
To gain access to new products or markets	To sell: • New products to existing customers • Existing products to new customers	Gaining access to new customers/markets	Cultural fit. Customer retention
As a substitute for R&D	To pick technology winners at an early stage of their market development and use superior resources to build a market position quickly	How much integration should there be?	Loss of talent
To create a new industry	To use a mix of existing and acquired resources to establish the means of competing in a new industry or continuing to compete in an industry whose boundaries are eroding	How to integrate? Which areas and to what extent?	Cultural fit Technical fit

Identify operational barriers to integration

For very practical reasons the acquirer may not want, or be able to, fully integrate the business it has acquired. Barriers to the level of desired integration need to be identified as early as possible so the negotiating and acquisition integration teams can assess their impact. Some significant operational barriers to integration are set out in Table 4.2 below:

Table 4.2	Operational barriers to acquisition integration
Barrier	*Comment*
Level of physical separation	Where the target company operates in a distant country or region it may be wise to maintain a higher than normal level of operational independence.
Structure of distribution channels	Where a target company is successfully serving customers through separate distribution channels it is probably sensible to maintain these independent channels, at least in the first instance.
Type of technology	If the target's technology is different to that of its new company there is a strong argument for allowing at least the core technical team to have some autonomy.
Type of operating systems	Similarly, where the operating systems (IT platforms) are complex, and incompatible with the parent company's systems it may make sense to retain functional independence, at least in the short term. Obviously key reporting systems must be aligned.
Demands of senior management and stakeholders	The deal structure (earn-out, minority stake etc) may require partial independence for an initial period. This should be factored into the negotiated price.
Legal constraints	Legal constraints may require the parent company to operate at arm's length within a particular market and maintain a high level of independence.
Public relations considerations	There may be a public relations requirement in certain markets and certain sectors to retain the acquired brand and independent operating units; again this needs to be factored into the negotiated price.

Operational integration barriers can increase the risk and even become 'deal-breakers'. It is a mistake to allow such operational barriers to pass largely unnoticed during negotiation, as they can become real problems later on.

Operational constraints will obviously affect the speed and depth of integration. Choices will have to be made about the way in which the target will be managed, ranging from allowing the target to have effective operating independence through partial integration to taking full control.

The acquirer should be clear about the type of parent it wants to be and the level of independence it will allow the acquired business. Table 4.3 below shows the options.

Table 4.3 **Level of integration options**

| Activity | Level of integration | | |
	Independence	*Partial*	*Full*
Budgeting	Effective autonomy	Clear guidelines	Integrated into company-wide policies
Investment appraisal	Guidelines on appraisal and funding	Company-wide policies followed, except for minor investments	Company-wide policies on all investments
Personnel	Fully independent	Broad guidelines	Company-wide policies and procedures
Marketing and sales	Fully independent	Clear guidelines on key areas such as brand and pricing	Company-wide policies
New product development	Limited coordination	Clear guidelines on key areas	Company-wide policies followed
Supplier base	No central supplier list	Key suppliers identified; terms negotiated	Supplier base fully integrated; centralised purchasing
Information technology	No common platforms	Common platforms in some key areas	Common platforms throughout
Legal framework	Independent entity	Many common systems	Common systems throughout

For most acquisitions, the ideal is to achieve full integration, though the speed at which this is achieved may be influenced by particular circumstances. It took Reed International and Elsevier Science about five years to integrate properly into Reed Elsevier. Broadly, the less the target is integrated, the greater the level of risk. Risks include failure to achieve cost savings, and conflicts on strategic direction, investment and sales and marketing or other policies.

Whilst taking control, acquirers should not forget that integration should be a two-way process. Acquirers are not perfect and acquired companies are not run by dummies. The best acquirers know that there may well be some tricks to learn from the business it is buying and that the integration policy and process must not be allowed to bury this value.

Minimise uncertainty

Change equals uncertainty. Uncertainty stems from the fact that the groups of people affected have a number of expectations but no idea of whether or not those expectations will be met. Their first concerns will be 'me' questions – 'what does this mean for me?' For the acquirer this means:

- Make people decisions early
- Communicate openly, honestly and a lot more than you think you have to

Make people decisions early

As the buyer you will have convinced yourself that you can run the business better and will be itching to get on with it. The first concern of those who you are going to rely on to make all those changes is: what does this mean for me? They all know that acquisitions mean job losses so where do you think their logic takes them? And having got there, is their next instinct to work productively and serve customers with a smile? People like certainty. Even if there are to be mass redundancies and closures it is best to say so up front and then get on and get them out of the way. Do not procrastinate; there is no 'right' time to make this sort of announcement. With it done at least everyone knows where they are. As long as restructuring is handled with sensitivity people will respond much better than they will to creeping, piecemeal changes. They only add to the anxiety.

Communicate openly

There should be no secrets, no surprises, no hype and no empty promises. This includes being able to say, 'we don't know' or 'we haven't decided yet'.

Whilst the acquirer may be pumping out a consistent message about how great the new world will be, this will not by any means be what everyone will be thinking. Figure 4.2 below outlines some of their concerns.

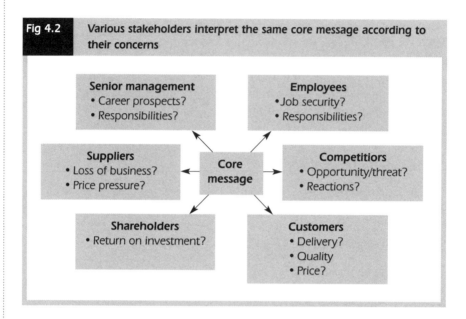

Fig 4.2 Various stakeholders interpret the same core message according to their concerns

This illustration shows that communication with stakeholders is complex. There must be a consistent core message. Underneath this, different messages are required for different audiences. Each one must be honest and accurate, but tailored to address the real concerns of real people.

Best practice in communication is to:

- Communicate early and often; avoid silence

- Communicate in a coherent and consistent manner

- Avoid contradictory messages; they destroy credibility and increase uncertainty

- Appoint a single person or small team to act as the focal point for the communication

- Develop specific messages to address the individual needs of each of the differing audiences

- Use the best communication tools, language and tone for each audience

- Listen to feedback; establish a two-way communication process

- Answer questions as honestly as possible – if you don't know, say so

- Be open about reasons for the acquisition and the likelihood of job losses
- Challenge false rumours

Remember that actions and non-verbal signals are very important and that a physical presence is the best way of confirming the written message.

Worst practice is for the message to get out in the wrong way. One British group forgot about time zones. It prepared a press release with a time of release embargo for the morning, but because it did not specify GMT in the UK, employees in Asia heard about the acquisition on the radio on the way into work. They immediately got on the phone to colleagues elsewhere in the world and the communication team had to back-pedal its way out of a mess.

Day-one communication

For the day-one announcement and explanation of the future, personal contact is best; this means individual or group meetings. They should be supported by useful documentation. Ideally this is a tailor-made presentation, which describes the acquirer and explains exactly what this will mean for the acquired company and particularly for its employees. In addition, the acquiring company should have sufficient copies of basic documents such as its:

- Company brochure
- Company annual accounts
- Terms and conditions of the company pension scheme
- Standard operating procedures where relevant

Acquired employees are often reassured once they are clear about future strategy, policies and procedures.

Be prepared for the obvious questions

The uncertainty surrounding an acquisition will manifest itself in 'what about me' questions such as:

- Will the combined company continue to employ me?
- Will I continue to work in the same place with the same colleagues?
- Is my workload about to increase?
- Will I have a new boss?
- Will I get the same level of current benefits?
- Will my potential future benefits be better or worse?
- Have my longer-term prospects for career development improved or got worse?

- Will my status change?
- Will my lifestyle change?

The questions and the emotions behind these questions will also change as the deal proceeds from its early days to full integration. The different emotions are shown in Table 4.4 below.

Table 4.4	Good people management during the first days depends on understanding employee emotions	
Event/action	*Employee emotion*	*Disaster avoidance*
Deal planned		Understand culture, motivations and priorities. Avoid rumours
News breaks	'Wow! We're being taken over!...'	Communicate clearly and effectively to everyone, immediately
News sinks in	'What does that mean for me?'	Check the right message actually sank in
First Monday	'So what happens now then?'	Clarify initial implications and changes
Operational intentions stated	'Is that change good for me?' 'Will it really happen?'	Understand perceived implications and any barriers to making things happen
First actions	'That is/is not what they [officially] said they would do'	Build trust through consistency
First operational problem	'I don't like that... things used not to be like this'	Deal with problems quickly and build confidence that they will not be repeated

If the acquirer does not act quickly and coherently, employees within both organisations will become increasingly unsettled. They will start to focus on their current situation and spend time doing things which are not much use, such as:

- Spreading rumours and listening to other people's rumours
- Trying to find out about any changes and the latest news
- Looking for a new job

Productivity declines and key employees leave. The pharmaceutical mergers of the 1990s saw the mass exodus of senior managers from many of the acquired companies. Remember that the true cost of replacing key employees is a significant proportion of their first year's salary. This takes into account productivity loss during recruitment, recruitment cost and low productivity of the replacement during induction. Put simply: the acquirer must get to the key employees early, with the right message.

Senior management from the acquirer should be involved because the people in the acquired business need to see and believe that the new parent takes them seriously: 'Well, the big boss did make the effort to come all the way from London to see us'. Therefore, senior management within the parent should be part of the communication team, on site, on day one even for minor acquisitions. They must be seen to be interested in the future of the new organisation.

As the day-to-day management of the acquisition has been delegated to the acquisition team, senior management can perform a vital role of 'management by walking about'; meeting employees, customers and suppliers to demonstrate their level of commitment to the smooth development of the new combined organisation.

Do not forget the customer

Uncertainty does not just exist internally. Customers have not necessarily been sitting around waiting for their supplier to be taken over. They are likely to react with scepticism and ask questions like 'will prices go up?' and 'will delivery change?' Do not forget that competitors will react to targeting accounts in the hope that the fee change has unsettled them.

Do not forget the power of symbolism

Sometimes painting the canteen is enough. Positive progress does not have to be with the big things, in fact progress can be tricky with the bigger things because they take too long to realise.

Treating those who will suffer through restructuring with respect and maintaining their dignity also sends powerful signals. This is a powerful way of showing what sort of company they are now working for.

Manage properly

Should we appoint an integration manager?

Yes, you should appoint an integration manager. Like any other big project you need one person accountable for the project's success otherwise there will be delay, false starts and confusion. Integration is a full-time job. It cannot be done part-time by, say, the buyer's MD or the MD of the relevant subsidiary. These people have a business to run and besides that they will concentrate on the urgent day-to-day issues. Nor should it be left to some bright MBA unless the integration is small and highly-structured. An integration manager needs to be a well-respected all-rounder who understands the industry, who knows his or her way round the acquiring company and who has the confidence of its senior management. Other skills and attributes will include:

- Proven experience in project management
- Effective interpersonal skills
- Sensitivity to cultural differences
- Ability to facilitate project groups

Ideally, the integration manager will be in the midstream of their career, with a broad experience while remaining receptive to 'new' and evolving business practices.

Effective integration requires clarity of purpose, detailed target setting and detailed reviews. Smaller acquisitions and private equity transactions require less integration than larger complex mergers such as that of HP and Compaq, but even the smallest 'stand-alone' transactions require a plan, if only to establish financial, operational and strategic reporting lines.

Role of the integration manager

The MD, not the integration manager, is accountable for the performance of the business. The integration manager acts like a consultant held accountable for the creation and delivery of the integration plan and reaching its milestones.

The integration team

Acquisition integration is like any other major project. It has a one-off objective, limited duration, financial or other limitations, complexity, potential risk and requires an inter-disciplinary approach. The integration team should therefore include members with both project management experience and operational skills. If the required experience or skills are not available, the acquirer should consider bringing in external resources such as consultants or interim managers.

Key managers must be selected as early as possible. They will then make decisions on additional assistance required during acquisition integration. The integration team should comprise a balance of different people and skills. At least some team members should have previous acquisition and integration experience.

As the probability of making the acquisition increases, the support provided to the acquisition team should increase. It is best to maintain continuity by adding additional team members to an existing structure. The level of additional resource required depends on the complexity of the acquisition, its strategic importance and its size. Experience suggests that in larger acquisitions, individuals should be assigned in at least six areas:

- Personnel
- Sales and marketing
- Production/service delivery
- Logistics
- Information technology
- Finance

Each of these areas will have specific and detailed tasks which should be broken down in detail, and then built into the overall master plan. If this all sounds a bit much, remember that resource requirements are frequently underestimated.

If outsiders are needed, they can be expensive, but remember always that their cost is insignificant in the context of an acquisition. The trade-off of more effective and more rapid integration against the cost of adding a few additional internal or external members to the team is often significant. Trying to muddle through with existing resources is short-sighted and often counter-productive.

Many executives fail to appreciate the scale of the merger task. Imagine bringing together two organisations that ostensibly mirror each other in size and function: two finance, marketing and research and development departments, two sets of manufacturing or retail sites, differing information technology and international operations. The numbers can be enormous: the aborted GE/Honeywell merger involved over 500,000 employees worldwide. Add to that the extra complexity of different countries, cultures, time zones and languages, and it becomes easier to see why so many acquisitions fail.

In the acquisition wave of the late 1990s, most successful mega-acquirers used external consultants to assist with implementation, which was considered a unique skill and process. There were additionally at the time few companies with the in-house expertise to undertake large-scale implementation on their own. Moreover, many employers felt they had insufficient manpower. After completing acquisitions it became clear that, even with consultants, the implementation phase required a large staff. One French banking mega-merger had 450 post-acquisition working-groups each averaging 10 employees. This equated to 4,500 executives working on implementation globally – even before they had accounted for consultants.

Increasingly, acquirers are bringing the implementation process in-house. Repeat acquirers such as Royal Bank of Scotland are hiring former consultants, among others, and building their own in-house expertise in acquisition. This trend is not just for multinational companies – smaller companies and those planning to acquire aggressively are also experimenting with in-house resources.

But why create a significant internal resource for something that happens only occasionally? In the long term, it may cost less than hiring consultants, who can charge up to £15 m a month for mega-acquisitions. It also offers companies greater control over the process. Over time, a company's internal M&A skills may become so well-honed that they become much more likely to make future deals succeed. In some cases acquisition implementation can become a source of competitive advantage.

Potential acquirers can choose to maintain a separate implementation team, as does GE Capital, though this is relatively rare. The team remains a separate entity and is called upon to integrate several acquisitions as they arise. It is the most expensive option and requires several acquisitions or other projects to take place over a year to justify the cost. But the company can usually ensure acquisitions are integrated quickly and smoothly.

Other acquirers, such as LaFarge, the French cement producer, have a small but separate M&A unit consisting of only a few individuals. It routinely oversees the integration of acquisitions and supplements its ranks with fellow employees or external advisers who work on specific tasks. By rotating employees on and off projects, it spreads acquisition expertise throughout the company, rather than refining it to a few key integration experts.

However the team is resourced, there should be enough skilled people on the ground from day one. Do not be tempted to add resources on an ad hoc basis. Once the team is in place, each member should prepare a detailed project plan for his specific area of operation. To do this they must be absolutely clear about what they need to do, and how their roles relate to the overall goals of the acquisition.

A properly structured and resourced induction plan therefore avoids throwing any new team members in at the deep end. They need to understand:

- The acquisition rationale and how it fits the overall company strategy
- The key drivers of success and failure of the acquisition
- Their specific role within the overall team and how this relates to the overall objective

- Who else is in the team and who to turn to for assistance
- Any bonuses available for on-target completion of the tasks

Prioritise what needs to be done

The integration manager will have the overall responsibility for coordinating the development and fine-tuning of the project plan. This will involve:

- Involvement with the negotiation team on the investment requirements to achieve required objectives
- Involvement in briefing the due diligence team on the key risk components
- Briefing senior management on task definition and resource requirements
- Delegating individual elements of the project plan to specific integration team members

Once the plan comes together, the integration manager has to decide what needs to be done in what order. As with most activities, 80 per cent of the wins will be generated by 20 per cent of the activities. Focusing on the projects which yield the highest financial impact in the shortest time has two benefits:

- It helps secure early wins. In contrast to the naive optimism of many top managers, the initial feeling on the part of both workforces is that it will not succeed. The only things that will get buy-in are well-communicated tangible wins to convince employees that there is a brighter future
- It helps shorten the process by completing the most important projects first

Traditionally the early effort focuses on reducing costs, but reducing costs often proves more difficult than first thought. What looks like a simple business of eliminating duplication and reducing unnecessary overhead always turns out to be a complex long term re-engineering job in which work processes and procedures are fundamentally reorganised, people are redeployed and additional investment in training is needed – oh, and everything has to be achieved with a demotivated workforce.

Depending on the extent of the integration, there is bound to be duplication and everyone internally will be aware of this. The best way forward is to deal with any such redundant effort then get on with capturing the longer-term growth-orientated benefits. Do not get hung up on cost savings for their own sake. They are a one-off. Once they have been realised there is nothing left. Growth, on the other hand, continues forever.

Get the reporting right

At each stage of the development of the pre- and post-acquisition plan, managers must maintain information systems, including a detailed checklist, and ensure it is completed at each stage. Some managers may choose to use project management software for this purpose. Software can help to integrate cash flow and resource demands and conflicts into a coherent and integrated action plan. Developing a coherent project plan also provides a framework for assessing risk profiles.

Without quality data it is impossible to monitor the integration process. The acquired company needs quickly to start reporting in the standard format.

Overlap with the due diligence team

All the evidence suggests that the most effective integration managers are those that serve on the due diligence team.

It is vital to have a dedicated group focusing purely on integration; it must not be distracted by other operational requirements. This focus will enable the group to:

• Research the market and the company and fully understand the target

• Ask the right questions of the due diligence providers

• Consider the operational problems that should be resolved following the deal

• Plan how to achieve the desired value-add

By understanding the operational and market dynamics of the acquisition in detail, the team will be able to evaluate and value the target. This quality of understanding and insight also strengthens the hand of the negotiating team.

If the integration team can hit the ground running and win the support of the acquired company, it can then implement change rapidly and avoid the immediate erosion of value.

Remember, though, that the integration and bid teams should be balanced as they perform different roles and the integration manager has different priorities to the negotiating team. His role is conciliatory and about building trust and value. It is not adversarial as that of the negotiating team can be, particularly when there is some tough deal-doing. Figure 4.3 illustrates these roles.

Some additional staff from the target company may join the team post acquisition. This will depend on the initial assessment of the acquired company's management teams and the personnel review, which is part of Week One activities. Acquisition planning should always be prepared for the worst case – that none or few of the target management will be suitable for key integration roles in the early post-acquisition stages.

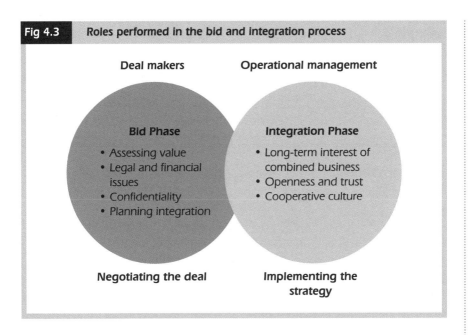

Fig 4.3 — Roles performed in the bid and integration process

Deal makers — Operational management

Bid Phase
- Assessing value
- Legal and financial issues
- Confidentiality
- Planning integration

Integration Phase
- Long-term interest of combined business
- Openness and trust
- Cooperative culture

Negotiating the deal — Implementing the strategy

Soft issues are paramount

Acquirers often find it difficult to see that cultural differences are significant barriers to progress and find it hard to accept that cultural barriers cannot be dismantled quickly or easily.

Identifying cultural barriers to integration

The culture of a company is the set of assumptions, beliefs and accepted rules of conduct that define the way things are done. These are never written down and most people in an organisation would be hard pressed to articulate just what the organisation's culture is. However, these rules and shared beliefs are powerful. It is a mistake for an acquirer to assume that the target company will have anything like the same cultural dynamics as the acquirer. Morrisons, a leading food retailer, blamed its post-acquisition performance dip on the culture clash with Safeway while Marks and Spencer took ten years to get to grips with Brooks Brothers' culture. It is very important for acquirers to spend time on understanding the way in which the personnel within the target company behave – both individually and within the 'culture' of the business. Management can then decide how it would like to see the target company's culture develop and, in the meantime, adapt the way it manages the target. Table 4.5 below summarises the main points to consider.

Table 4.5	Areas of cultural difference to be assessed
Area	*Difference to consider between acquirer and target*
Structure	Is responsibility and authority very different?
Staff	Does it employ many more people to carry out similar tasks?
Skills set	Does it have a lower emphasis on the importance of skills development within the organisation
(Management) style	Is there a different emphasis on the way tasks are carried out (some typical broad divisions are bureaucratic, authoritarian, and democratic)?
Shared values	Is there a common set of beliefs within the organisation as to how it should develop and what are they?
Systems	Does the target go about recruitment, appraisal, motivation, training and discipline in a very different way?
Reporting	How disciplined, formal and financial are reporting procedures?

Information will have to be collected from various sources to understand what is important:

- Management interviews (if access is granted)
- Relevant experts if the acquisition is in a new country/sector
- Trade literature and website visits
- Ex-employees (through contacts and due diligence if possible)
- Customers (through contacts and due diligence if possible)
- Suppliers (through contacts and due diligence if possible)
- Mystery shopping (acting as a prospective customer and analysing responses)

It is also useful to remember that culture tends to reflect the business model, so it therefore makes sense to understand and reflect on differences between the two companies' business models while assessing their cultures.

The ideal integration pattern is to achieve a seamless transition between the old organisation (parent) and the new (parent plus target) so that the new organisation can work with a single purpose, a single set of operating characteristics and so on. Failure to do this leads to at least some of the following consequences:

- Increased labour turnover
- Loss of skilled staff

- Reduced productivity
- Damaged labour relations
- Strikes
- Public relations problems

Cultural convergence is rarely achieved quickly and sometimes not at all. Operational and cultural barriers hinder progress. People within an organisation learn to accept its working practices over time. We rarely have the luxury of several months or years with an acquisition. Changes need to be made quickly. This reinforces the need to concentrate only on essential changes and those which will have a significant impact in the short term.

Adjust integration to fit the cultural gap

If a target has a significantly different culture, this can substantially increase post-acquisition costs or hold back performance. The risk increases if the businesses are to be merged as opposed to operating as independent units.

The acquirer needs to assess the impact of the cultural divide and plan accordingly. Where there is a big cultural gap between the two organisations:

- The pace of many aspects of integration should be slowed down
- The acquirer's management may have to spend more time with the business
- The level of integration may be revised down, at least for the first 6–12 months
- The new parent should explain in detail why certain changes must be made and not just inflict them without consultation unless absolutely necessary
- Company training levels may have to be enhanced
- Various standardised operating procedures may need to be introduced and enforced
- Additional financial resources may need to be budgeted for

Get people to work together

The best way to overcome cultural problems is to get people working together to solve problems. Short-term projects that focus on achieving results quickly involving employees from both companies almost always serve to bridge the cultural gap.

Get the managers to communicate rather than communications professionals because they will not just say the words but engage in a dialogue too.

The integration plan

With the expanded team, the final stages of the integration plan can be completed. In outline, this consists of three phases, as shown in Table 4.6.

Table 4.6	Integration phases
Phase	*Activity*
Day One/Week One	Clear communication to employees and other stakeholders.
	Immediate and urgent items required to ensure that key elements of control are transferred smoothly and efficiently.
The 100-day plan	Introduction of any major changes in operating and personnel practices.
Year one	Introduction of additional procedures and longer-term staff and business development practices.

Speed is important

As we have already seen, before walking through the door of its new prized asset, the acquiring company must know how it is going to manage integration. Once inside the business, it must then put its plan into action. To recap, the reasons put forward for speed are the:

• Need to reduce employees' uncertainty quickly

• Advantage of capitalising on momentum; playing on the expectation of change

• Need to return managers to their original jobs, avoiding an 'army of occupation'

• Need to show results; quickly justifying the acquisition

Any factors that lessen the need for full speed should already have been analysed and their impact built in to the integration plan. In any acquisition, there are three areas, which require early attention. They are:

• Ensuring that the acquirer gains complete financial control of the operation

• Communicating effectively with all the stakeholders of the acquired business

• Managing the expectations of all involved

Day One

The first day of a new acquisition is crucial. On Day One the acquirer should plan to complete a series of essential actions during the day and then review progress at the end of the day. The acquirer's soft and hard objectives for the day include:

- Gaining control
- Showing that the acquirer means business
- Showing that the acquirer cares about the target
- Winning the hearts and minds of the new employees
- Providing clear guidelines about how the next stages will develop

Also from Day One the acquirer must secure what it has brought. This means ensuring that the new acquisition will start to provide value to the new enlarged organisation. Day One actions affect the development of key tangible and intangible assets, including:

- People
- Products
- IPR
- Plant
- Premises
- Customers
- Suppliers

Every member of the post-acquisition team will have clear targets to achieve on Day One. The acquirer needs to follow the post-acquisition plan closely. There is no time to discuss what needs to be done – this has all been planned, discussed and reviewed prior to the acquisition. The acquirer needs to take action rapidly, calmly and in a systematic manner.

At the end of Day One, the integration team should review progress against the Day One action plan. Any additional actions, which become necessary during the next stages of the integration can be agreed.

Financial control

It is essential that financial control passes from the acquired company to the parent at once. This ensures that:

- Potential liabilities are limited to those existing at the time of acquisition
- The company has time to verify financial management procedures in the acquired company and review security procedures
- The ownership of assets is immediately clarified

Obviously much of the groundwork will have been covered doing due diligence. With the right preparation and resources, harmonising financial controls should be relatively straightforward.

Week One

Creating clear targets for the Week One review forces the pace of reform – and ensures that the acquirer has a defined position from which any additional corrective action can be taken to ensure that targets are met. Week One will see the completion of a number of tasks which will shape the structure of the organisation. At the end of Week One the acquirer needs to have:

- Completed the initial communication plan to all stakeholders
- Completed the personnel review and confirmed the new company structure
- Started the consultation process on any redundancies
- Gained complete commercial control of the organisation
- If not already done, established clearly what action needs to be taken to further integrate the company's:
  - Management structure
  - Financial management
  - Personnel management and development
  - Legal compliance including health and safety
  - Quality control systems
  - Information systems
  - Marketing and customer interface

While following its plan and avoiding the temptation to dither, the team must spot and assess unforeseen barriers to integration as early as possible. It will also need to be on the look-out for any adaptations to the plan needed to accommodate what they have found out on the ground.

Month One

The Month One review is an important step towards the successful conclusion of integration. At this stage the acquirer needs to review progress and identify bottlenecks.

Typically the Month One review will cover the following areas in considerable detail:

- Management quality and stability
- Customer contracts and pricing structures
- Logistics evaluation
- Sales force evaluation and future plan
- Marketing planning
- Integration of Customer Relationship Management (CRM) functions with parent company
- Stock holding
- Plant analysis and maintenance
- Product analysis; in-house versus sub-contracting
- Supplier base
- Asset analysis
- Information and reporting systems
- Contingency plan

Whilst there will always be the need to focus on the immediate, for example a problem with a key customer, this should not be at the expense of this thorough review. Maintaining a structured methodology with tasks, timelines and milestones will continue to ensure that there is a clear integration roadmap. The target remains to achieve the planned gains. The entire post-acquisition team, plus relevant senior management from the new company should attend the review. Set aside a full day and meet off-site to avoid distractions.

One hundred days

All major decisions should be completed within 100 days. One hundred days is perhaps an arbitrary time frame but it is put forward by a host of writers and consultants as a turning point in the integration. Private equity investors tend to find that at this stage they can forecast the likely success of their investments. The first one or two board meetings will have taken place and the immediate financial performance of the business will be visible.

By this time, the acquirer should have signed off on:

- Organisational structure, manpower requirements
- Personnel development, compensation structures
- Location decisions
- Asset management, maintenance
- Product range decisions
- Company procedures
- Financial management
- Current supplier agreements and how they are going to be changed
- Customer agreements, channel and pricing policies

By the end of 100 days the acquirer should be in the position to confirm the potential savings and benefits that will come from the acquisition. Senior management can respond to the implications of this information, and if necessary instigate new company-wide initiatives.

Continual updating of the project plan reduces the uncertainty surrounding the achievement of the 100-day target. Where tasks are slipping outside their initial planned duration, the team leader can decide to increase resources or deal with areas of conflict within the company.

Each of the divisional leaders within the acquisition team has their own responsibilities laid down in the project plan. These need to be regularly reviewed and then presented at a formal meeting at the end of the 100-day period.

An acquisition is a time of great stress. Having been through the process it is a good idea to codify the lessons learnt so that next time the people involved have the benefit of the company's acquired experience. For this reason, roughly twelve months after the deal is signed, make time for a post-acquisition review.

Post-acquisition review

The acquisition review allows everyone involved in the acquisition to assess and learn. It is vital for acquirers to learn about what went right or wrong in the acquisition process. Even the most experienced acquirers will make mistakes, but it is foolhardy to repeat those already made elsewhere.

The post-acquisition review will affect the value that an acquirer will put on future acquisitions. It should gain valuable insights into the way in which it:

- Develops an acquisition rationale
- Values a prospective target
- Researches a prospective target
- Negotiates an acquisition
- Plans post-acquisition activities
- Implements its post-acquisition plan

As it is so valuable, the acquirer should be prepared to put aside sufficient time and resources to ensure that the review is done properly. It will take a lot of time and effort, so it is best organised by the relevant board member. It should include all key players in the acquisition – the acquisition team, negotiators, due diligence providers, board members and so on.

Ideally everyone involved should produce a review document for circulation prior to an open discussion. The group can then:

- Compare the various stages of the project plan to actual events and assess the impact of major variances
- Capture the lessons learnt in a formal acquisition 'guidelines' document

What the review provides is a mechanism for making better judgements about future acquisitions. From identifying whether initial assumptions were correct, to the actions that the acquirer took to convert the theory into reality, these all help to improve the performance of future acquisitions. Experience shows that the return on investment of this type of review can be very significant.

It is the board's job to ensure that the lessons of the past acquisition are formally integrated into the standard acquisition document and that the analysis is added to the company literature concerning acquisition.

Acquisition guidelines

A systematic planning process increases the odds of a successful acquisition. People planning the deal need accurate and consistent information about integration. They should not be 'reinventing the wheel' when time is short. Bespoke guidelines can also help when selecting and managing consultants, helping to ensure they operate within the company's parameters without duplicating work.

Guidelines must be flexible enough to cover various types of acquisitions and different degrees of integration. For instance, a foreign subsidiary acquisition operating in a stand-alone capacity may require more input from the finance and IT departments. Conversely, a full merger of two operations may need more attention from HR over employment legislation and communication and cultural matters.

Acquisition guidelines should be revisited after each acquisition and the necessary changes made to the structure of the plan, its reporting and evaluation methodology. The acquirer should use the post-acquisition review to learn the key successes and failures. These must be incorporated into the acquisition guidelines. This 'library' will be a growing resource which will give those individuals new to acquisition and acquisition planning a vital resource to improve their understanding of what needs to be planned and implemented and how to overcome problems.

As the integration manager has now inevitably moved on to other responsibilities, it is important that the responsibility for the review and upgrading of the standard operating procedures towards post-acquisition integration should be maintained at the highest level within the organisation.

Conclusion

Start thinking about integration right at the beginning of the process. We argue above that it is impossible to value a business without a pretty good idea of where the synergies will come from and how they will be captured, so it would be highly unprofessional not to have thought about integration right at the outset. As important is the body of evidence which tells us that the major cause of acquisition failure is poor integration. Doing the deal may be sexier, but integration is where the real money is made or lost. For goodness sake, too, make sure due diligence is structured to help with integration and not solely slanted towards completing the deal. Integration requires a completely different approach to transacting, thus it needs a separate team with its own leader who is responsible for progress. But that team must work closely with the deal team. Indeed it is highly likely that some individuals will be involved in both the transaction and the resulting integration.

Integration needs to be quick, but, apart from putting together a detailed plan of action, the main concern of the integration team should be to identify and deal with the soft issues which may act as a drag on quick and successful integration. Finally, once the dust has settled, learn from the experience. Carrying out a post-acquisition review introduces a typical planning loop into acquisitions, namely: do something, learn about it, incorporate the results.

Investigating the target   5

You have found the ideal target, spent a long time convincing your board and financiers that it is a good buy; you have given serious thought to what you are going to do with it once it is yours and you have managed to get the seller to agree to sell. This is where it starts to get scary. How do you know that this really is what the owner cracks it up to be? How do you know it is the seller's to sell? How do you know it does not have the corporate equivalent of dry rot? How can you be sure that all the plans you have to recoup that fancy price you are about to pay are realistic? The prospect of having to part with hard cash focuses the mind like nothing else can and one of the things you will most definitely want to do now is check out your intended purchase while you can still change your mind. In the trade this checking-out is called due diligence.

What is due diligence about?

Due diligence is not just about looking for black holes or skeletons in the cupboard. Although really it includes both of these, it should be carried out with the aim of making the deal successful. Due diligence is about three things:

- Checking that the target company is as presented to you and what you think you are buying
- Confirming the value you have put on the business
- Filling the gaps in your integration plan

When should you do it?

For a due diligence investigation to be meaningful it must be conducted before a buyer is committed to a deal. Figure 5.1 illustrates the typical process of an acquisition.

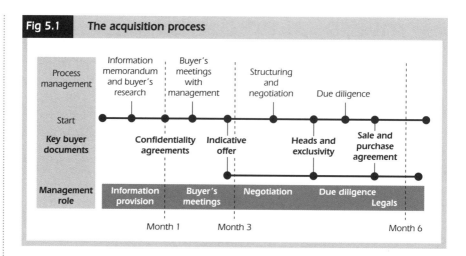

Fig 5.1 The acquisition process

Due diligence is usually conducted after Heads of Terms have been signed, because that signals that both sides are serious about continuing. The buyer therefore has every reason to believe that the time and money spent on due diligence will not be wasted. At this point a buyer typically enters into a period of exclusivity for 8–16 weeks.

There is no need to start all investigations at the same time. It is often best to kick off the commercial investigation as soon as possible because it can have an impact on the rest of the process. The legal investigations are started once some of the initial commercial and financial findings have become clear.

Be prepared for obstacles

Do not think that a buyer's willingness to sell will make due diligence easy. This is a typically Anglo-Saxon process and the relationship between buyer and seller is a dynamic mix of shared and opposed interests. The seller has no duty of care to the buyer so it is in the buyer's interest to have as much information as possible before being bound. Precisely the opposite applies to the seller because information means power. Sellers, and in particular their advisers who often do not get paid unless the transaction completes, are keen to see a rapid completion, so they set a tight timetable. Other legal systems resolve the buyer/seller conflict in different ways. Generally, in continental Europe the buyer has to commit on the basis of a less thorough investigation, but the seller does owe a duty of care.

Time pressure is being exacerbated by a number of factors. Sellers are tending to grant shorter periods of exclusivity. Increasingly sellers will only release information once the acquirer has signed a confidentiality agreement. These

agreements are becoming more and more onerous. They can take time to negotiate, holding up the due diligence exercise. Even with a confidentiality agreement
in place, the seller may wish to hold back sensitive commercial information for
the first part, or even all of the process. Some sellers even initiate a 'contract race'.

Remember, there is not a timetable in the world that cannot be extended for
a serious buyer.

The seller may wish to keep the proposed sale confidential from employees. If
this includes top management, or if the seller decides that top management
should not be interviewed for any other reason, then it makes due diligence very
difficult. The seller may prevent any personal visits to the target's premises, but
orchestrate a management presentation during which the buyer can meet the
team. It is only with the involvement of top executives that the acquirer can
obtain much of the information it needs about the business. If the access is too
limited, or the management presentation is too tightly stage-managed, the
acquirer should be prepared to walk away.

Finally, the acquirer should ask the seller whether the target company is
bound by any confidentiality obligations to third parties. These might exist, for
example, as a consequence of joint venture or other partnership agreements.
They may prevent the target company disclosing critical business information
without the partner's agreement.

Remember: the target will have prepared

Corporate finance advisers are highly motivated to complete transactions; this
inevitably means that they will have coached their clients on how best to present their business. They know that companies for sale can be made more
attractive and achieve a better price through some judicious grooming. You
should also bear in mind that any saleable company is likely to receive one or
more unsolicited approaches from prospective purchasers each year which
means that if a company puts itself up for sale, the timing is probably right.

Preparation or grooming can take months or even a couple of years. The
amount done depends on the time available in which to do it. The following is
a list of the areas that might have been covered before a buyer gets a close look
at the business.

Selecting the right buyers

The 'right' buyer is one who can complete quickly for the best price. A lot of the
value added by corporate finance comes from them finding purchasers with the
most to gain from the transaction, thus securing the best deal for the seller. A
good adviser will have selected no more than five to ten possible purchasers

from its extensive investigations. If you get to exclusivity, you will be one of the strongest candidates from those initially selected. However, any well-advised seller will keep at least one buyer in reserve after exclusivity has been granted, just in case.

Trading record

A company for sale needs to provide a demonstrable opportunity for sustained medium-term profit growth. If grooming starts early enough it is possible to manipulate sales, and profit, for example by delaying invoices over a year-end or carefully timing items of major expenditure, so that the seller can show the gently rising trend beloved of acquirers. Provisions will have been carefully renewed. There is no point in a seller just releasing excessive provisions all in one go because a buyer will simply not include them in its valuation. Excessive provisions will have been slowly released over a few years.

On top of this, you can bet that everything possible has been done to maximise profit in the current and preceding financial year. Although sellers know that buyers are paying for the future, they also know that the forecast for this year plus last year's actuals are going to play a major part in the valuation. One recent transaction went no further than the first day of due diligence because the accountants found out that the target company had no forward orders despite the fact that the buyer fully understood that this was a business with a lumpy order book. Other deals have been terminated when buyers discovered that major contracts had been lost, even though there was every chance that the lost business would be recouped fairly quickly.

Any seller will defer discretionary expenditure that does not have a payback before completion. Office walls will remain unpainted and the carpets threadbare. One engineering company managed to delay repairing its factory roof prior to sale by placing netting underneath to catch the falling glass. Other costs which can be reduced over the short term include advertising, not replacing staff who leave, taking non-working relatives off the payroll, keeping personal expenses to the absolute minimum, not starting costly R&D projects and not setting up new ventures that have little prospect of breaking even before completion. Any non-business costs will be avoided.

A pre-sale price rise may be another means of improving the trading record, especially if prices have not been reviewed for some time. A leading supplier of art materials had reviewed its prices six months before due diligence and under the guise of introducing consistency of pricing across a range of some 6,000 items, managed to increase prices by stealth by something like twice the rate of inflation. There was no way another across-the-board price rise could be contemplated for some time to come as customer perceptions were that the target's prices were high relative to the market, albeit without fully understanding how this state of affairs had come about.

Finally, the seller and its advisers should have reviewed accounting policies so that the buyer does not have an excuse to revise profits, and therefore price, downwards by adjusting any policy which inflates profit while ignoring those that do not.

Forecasts

The seller should have put together a forecast for the next two years' profit and cash flow. The current year forecast will be presented in great detail and will be achievable. Forecasts will not normally be unrealistically high because a failed sale damages value but, however, sellers will be looking for the best possible price and will therefore assess the synergies available to each prospective purchaser and put a value on its own rarity value, if any. The seller will also be aware of industry rules-of-thumb.

As a final means of talking up the future, vendors will be coached to look at the deal from the buyer's perspective. As a result they will normally be ready to volunteer their thoughts on achievable cost savings – not out of altruism but with the aim of sharing them.

Installing control systems

Companies for sale will want to give the appearance of being efficiently run and well controlled. Sellers know that prospective purchasers will want to compare monthly budgeted performance with actual performance over the last three years. Once a business decides to sell, therefore, it will need to put a system of budgets and monthly management accounts in place if they do not already exist.

Reducing business risks

Businesses which rely on a small number of customers or suppliers increase their risk of losing sales, suddenly running short of materials or being squeezed on cost. An essential part of pre-sale grooming is to diversify these risks by finding new customers, new lines of business and new sources of supply. Due diligence should concern itself with the robustness of such relationships. An example of a case where this had not been done, and which came close to scuppering a deal, was a company which relied on two raw materials. Demand for its own products was suddenly booming because the market had underestimated the effects of new legislation. What the target company had not done was to secure a sufficient supply of raw materials. This was against a background where raw materials suppliers had spent years waiting for a price rise which never came and their patience was now exhausted. Old plant was being decommissioned rather than modernised. The result was that the demand/supply balance was tightening very quickly. If demand continued on its present trajectory raw materials would be rationed, thus denying the target its ability to capitalise on its growing market. Fortunately, the target was of sufficient standing to be able to secure sufficient raw material, but it was a close run thing.

Management and staff

Depending on the acquirer and reasons for the deal, tying in the right management to the target company can be the most important factor in a deal going ahead. Before the company is officially put up for sale, the seller should have done all it could to present a stable and committed management team. If it is a business that has relied on the disproportionate talents of one person, usually the founder, who is not going to continue with the business once it has been sold, strenuous efforts will have been made over an extended time frame to hand the day-to-day running of the business to the next generation. If this is not the case buyers should wonder what strength and depth there is in the management team.

The founder of a publishing business claimed that he arrived at ten every day and left before lunch, only coming in to open the mail. According to him, the business no longer needed him and his wife was giving him considerable 'ear-ache' because in her view he should have been spending as much time as possible with his young family. Common sense told the would-be buyer that this was not the whole truth. Why did he insist on opening the mail? Why could this not be delegated to his PA? The answer was he was the only person in the company who had a view of the big picture and opening the mail made sure he kept things this way. Furthermore the business was highly dependent on a large and unstable sales force. The founder's biggest contribution to the business was sales force recruitment and training – activities which took place on a sufficiently irregular basis for it to seem he was only there between 10 am and 1 pm every day. The reality was that he would also have a week of frantic activity and long hours every quarter or so. Finally, there was no management team beneath him. Contracts were administered by a secretary, the finance director was part-time and that was the extent of second-tier management.

Even with a strong management team tied in when a deal is done, it is a sad fact that the majority of them will have departed within two years of the transaction. This is why sellers are encouraged by their advisers to strengthen the second management tier as well as strengthening the top team.

Valuing assets

Buyers will value the business on its prospects. Non-business and surplus assets will have zero value in their eyes. The well-advised seller will make sure all underutilised and redundant assets, including investments, are sold off. Surplus land and freehold properties are the most obvious candidates for disposal but a looming sale removes the case for holding onto any assets on the off-chance that they might come in handy one day. It also frees up space which can be presented to prospective purchasers as giving room for expansion. Any stocks which are fully written down should be disposed of. These too are surplus assets which have zero value to the buyer.

There will usually be differences between the value of assets on the balance sheet and their market value. A seller will be advised to have assets revalued to avoid either underselling or 'pound for pound' adjustments by a buyer whose own revaluations suggest that assets are overvalued. This applies to working capital too. To avoid the risk of having to pay for missing working capital on a pound-for-pound basis, sellers will have reviewed:

- Stock provisions
- Old debts which might never be paid
- Bad debt provisions

They may also have paid a special dividend to strip out any surplus cash. As far as a seller is concerned, surplus cash will only be valued at face value and may not be valued at all if a buyer values the target on the basis of profit.

Tidying up legal and administrative matters

Enhancing a business in the eyes of prospective purchasers will mean all the legal loose ends should have been tidied up. This would include tidying up group structure, trying to clear up all outstanding litigation, registering trademarks and patents, formalising the contractual position of key staff, checking that the deeds to property are properly registered and that there are going to be no problems with leases over dilapidations. Tax affairs should also be sorted out as soon as a sale is mooted and, if they are not, any buyer has to ask how efficient the target really is. Finally, this might also be the perfect time to buy in minority or joint venture interests if the reasons for either of them have outlived their usefulness.

Sellers will be encouraged to get bad news on the table early on because they know that the earlier unattractive features are revealed, the less impact they will have on the deal.

Conclusion

Given sufficient time and high-calibre people, sellers will arrange the target's affairs in order to maximise the sale price. This is not to say that a buyer cannot find areas of weakness but it does mean that if they are to be found they will not necessarily be in the most obvious places.

How do I know what due diligence to do?

There are three main areas of due diligence, commercial, financial and legal and a host of sub-specialisms such as tax and pensions. Table 5.1 sets out areas which would typically be covered by different types of due diligence.

Table 5.1	Types of due diligence		
DD Type	*Commercial*	*Financial*	*Legal*
Focus	• Market • Customers • Future performance	• Business systems • Valuation • Tax	• Contracts • Assets • Warranties and indemnities • Sale and purchase agreements
Timing	Week 1–4 of exclusivity	Week 1–6 of exclusivity	Week 4–8 of exclusivity
Advisers	CDD specialists Market or strategy consultants	FDD specialists, typically linked to audit firms	Legal adviser, with specific M&A experience
Sub-areas	• Management • Technical/operational	• Pensions • IT • Fraud	• Pensions • Tax • Property • Environment

There is no right answer to the question of how much due diligence to do. In practice, time, money and the seller's patience will limit how much you do. You cannot investigate everything, so there is always a risk that you will not cover something that you should have. However, knowing that you can only cover the high points should force you to think about the areas which are the biggest potential risks to a successful transaction. Then you can get the maximum return from due diligence. The worst thing is to grind through the 'normal procedures' without understanding what you are trying to achieve.

A myriad of topics may be interesting or useful to cover; but the trick is to focus on what actually matters. That means following the links from your strategy, through the business case for the acquisition, to the factors which will drive or impede the future performance of the acquisition target, both alone and in its combination with its new parent. Experienced acquirers do this and put irrelevant topics to one side. Less perennial acquirers can fall into the trap of trying to 'find out everything' about the business and then, exhausted by the process, confusing themselves on the detail.

Preparation way before the process starts is a big help. If the acquirer has tracked the market sector and the target over a number of years it is far better equipped to focus on the key issues and move quickly and effectively in the due diligence phase.

Who does due diligence?

The short answer is that you are going to end up employing a host of specialist and expensive advisers, which only goes to underline the point made above about thinking very carefully about what you need.

It is usual for an acquirer to follow through from its original investigations and conduct some of its own due diligence in those areas which it is particularly well-placed to investigate. But acquirers usually also need to use outside advisers because:

- Conducting due diligence is a specialist skill and much can be gained by using advisers who spend all their time doing this type of work. They will do the work more quickly, are more likely to dig out hidden information, and know how to minimise disruption to the target company. They should be able to spot difficulties in advance and find ways around them. For example, this could be obtaining hard-to-get information or persuading busy or difficult management teams to cooperate. Experienced and competent advisers will also help to define the scope and then to review it as the process proceeds

- Advisers bring extra resources. Most acquirers simply do not have skilled resource sitting around on the off-chance of a deal

- The buyer needs to concentrate on the big picture. Subcontracting most of the detailed due diligence work means a buyer can focus on the really important issues. Remember that the disaster that was British and Commonwealth's purchase of Atlantic Computers was caused precisely because no-one did have an overview of due diligence

- The management of the target company may be reluctant to allow access to managers from a competitor or a threatening new entrant. They may be more prepared to deal with an independent professional firm

- The dangers of 'deal fever' were mentioned in Chapter 1. Advisers are independent and much less emotionally attached to a deal. It is possible to obtain many of the specialisms listed in Table 5.1 from one source, say one of the large accounting firms. One of the reasons for not doing so is the need for a range of opinions (another is that they are actually not very good outside their core disciplines)

Whilst subcontracting parts of the due diligence almost always makes sense, the acquirer must stay in close contact with various teams. The advisers can benefit from the inputs of their clients and provide input to their strategic thinking and integration planning. Obviously this is very difficult to do at the last minute; it is better to line up internal resources and external advisers in advance.

What do I do?

Next in importance, after knowing what you want, comes knowing from whom you are going to get it, in what form and when. Then you manage the process to make sure it arrives as planned.

Besides managing the seller, the buyer needs to deploy the strongest possible project management skills. There are numerous strands for the acquirer to coordinate, everyone on both sides of the transaction is busy and there is never enough time in the deal timetable, but the various elements of due diligence must be 'joined-up' and tie coherently into the forecasts, the business plan and into the integration plan. External advisers must be kept on track. Commercial, financial and legal due diligence teams need their efforts coordinating and each team's work needs continually adjusting in the light of new information. Above all, the buyer needs to make sure there is enough time to digest the information and analysis before making decisions. This is not some clever strategic, legal or financial exercise: it is unadulterated project management.

Get the right team

The right team can make the difference between an excellent due diligence process and something that costs a lot of money to tell you what you already know. Appendix B contains a checklist on working with advisers.

Team members need experience and a mix of business, investigative and analytical skills. Some investors look for sector experience above all else: this is wrong because definitions of sectors are so wide as to be useless in screening prospective advisers. Besides, having someone in a firm with relevant sector experience is no guarantee that he or she will have the right skills for your deal. Due diligence is a process which can be applied to any sector in any industry. In order of importance, therefore, the most important attributes to look for are:

- Experience of preparing due diligence reports
- Experience of the purchaser and a common understanding of objectives
- Experience of the target company's sector

Although the reputation of the firm is important, the individual qualities of the team are most important. You are going to look to these individuals for good advice in a period of great stress. If time permits, it is a good idea to meet the advisers' teams and satisfy yourself as to the level of their experience and how they would handle the assignment. Find out how much involvement the senior adviser will have. All too often the senior will 'sell' the work then disappear and leave more junior members to complete it. Given the points above you will also want to discuss the team leader's due diligence experience and perhaps knowledge of the sector under investigation.

When looking for lawyers, it is also advisable to look for creativity and to probe their record of suggesting sensible, commercial, solutions to problems. For example one law firm set out to assess the top 50 of a target company's 400 major contracts which were provided in a data room. Its team of juniors religiously copied out all the details of 50 contracts. The acquirer pointed out that there were simply four contract models which the target company used and which had evolved over time. All the LDD team had to do was set out the contract types and then note the exceptions.

This is not a precise science. Acquirers tend to select advisers based on whom they know and with whom they are comfortable. But to succeed the acquirer needs to assemble the right team.

Brief them properly

To state the obvious, if advisers do not know what you want from them, you are unlikely to get it. Formal letters of engagement can stipulate exactly what work will be carried out and define the costs which will be incurred while also confirming what is expected of the professionals and who will be responsible for regulating the information flow. Also make sure that you explain clearly what you want. Don't get tied up in jargon.

As well as understanding what is expected of them, they must also understand the wider issues such as:

- *Who else is advising?* Tax is a favourite area for duplication. It can be tackled by the lawyers or by the accountants. If you do not specify which, they will both try to cover it and you will end up with each commenting on the other's work at your expense

- *Reasons for the deal.* In one financial due diligence exercise the senior partner involved got very excited when he spotted a downward sales trend in one product line. Before setting off to investigate the reasons he told the client of his insightful discovery. The client knew already and was not in the least concerned as it was his own product range which was picking up the lost share

- *Areas of greatest worry.* As mentioned above, there is not time to cover everything. You must make sure advisers cover the areas of greatest perceived risk

- *Areas of sensitivity.* Due diligence is a fraught time for both sides. The last thing you want are your advisers upsetting the other side by, for example, insisting on talking to customers with whom they are in the middle of sensitive contract negotiations

- *Acceptable risks and materiality limits.* The chances are that you do not want every potential risk to be brought to your attention or included in the report

- *Structure of the deal.* There is a huge difference in the approach to due diligence between an assets deal and a share deal

- *Timetable.* Time is always tight and everyone must know when their due dates are. It is not clever to give false deadlines; by squeezing days out of an adviser's process you are limiting their thinking time and ability to give you insight

- *What is needed at the end – 400 pages or four?* Advisers know that they cannot be sued for providing too much information. On the other hand, the average non-exec reads his board papers between the car park and the board room on his way to the meeting. If you need a four-page summary of the highlights, say so.

Get the written report presented

The presentation gives you the chance to look the consultants in the eyes and get them to give you the answers they may have hedged in the report. You also want their opinions. If you have hired the right team, you will have a group of highly-experienced business analysts who have crawled over many different transactions. Their experience is what you are paying for.

Other points to watch

Be sensitive

Particularly in private companies and countries where the acquisition process is less well understood, management can be sensitive to due diligence. They may challenge whether it is needed at all – 'don't you trust me?' Experienced acquirers and their advisers can often win round the seller. They can argue that their investigation will allow the buyer to understand the full value of the business. Equally if a bank will be providing debt, they can point out that full due diligence is a requirement of the lending bank.

Any buyer is well advised to avoid disruption to the target business if only because it might come back and bite. As due diligence processes become more detailed and ever more onerous, they can impact the business negatively. If top management has to attend meetings which add no value to the business and focus on responding to the myriad of information requests, they are unable to deal with customers and other operational challenges. One reason for acquirers to be disappointed by post-deal trading can simply be that the management of the target company had taken its eye off the ball over the preceding weeks and months.

Remember your duty of confidentiality...

The acquirer has a duty of confidentiality implied by English law and on top there will typically be a formal confidentiality agreement. An acquirer who misuses confidential information could be sued for damages or an injunction issued to stop his use of the information.

...and promises you have made...

These may include promises not to solicit any of the target's customers or employees. They usually bite not only during the due diligence period but also for a stated period after an abortive transaction.

...and the perils of insider dealing

If either the acquirer's or the seller's securities are traded on the London Stock Exchange or other securities market, then the proposed transaction may be price-sensitive. Insiders should neither deal in the securities nor discuss the transaction with third parties who are likely to deal in the securities until the transaction is made public and is no longer price-sensitive.

Commercial due diligence

Commercial due diligence (CDD) is the investigation of a company's market, competitive position and prospects. It is an investigation which covers its products, relationships with customers, distributors and suppliers, and to some extent management and operations. It should provide a clear view of the company's future which can be fed into financial analysis and valuation.

Why should I carry out both commercial and financial due diligence?

In short because you will get a different perspective. Remember what was said earlier. Due diligence is not just about confirming assets and rooting out hidden liabilities. The success of a deal is going to rely on the target's performance in the market and CDD is one of the few due diligence disciplines that gets its information from that market.

Financial due diligence (FDD) teams focus internally. They analyse the financial records and speak at length with the company's management. After some contact with management, it usually starts with secondary sources (i.e. desk research) and carries on to use primary sources, i.e. enquiries among people who are actively involved in the market, or who observe it closely such as customers, distributors, specifiers, regulators, suppliers, competitors, and former employees.

CDD and FDD should be seen as complementary activities, both looking to understand the target's sustainable profit from different angles. The two work programmes should be coordinated and culminate in jointly agreed forecasts. The two teams should communicate freely with each other because their different perspectives can open up new lines of enquiry and because each have access to information which can be valuable to the other. For example, the FDD team may have easy access to lists of former customers and perhaps former employees. The CDD team could obtain this information themselves, but it would take longer. Similarly, the CDD team can obtain a more precise view of market size, segmentation and future growth rates than accountants; the FDD team can plug this information into their forecasts and scenarios.

What is the CDD process and where does the information come from?

The commercial due diligence process is set out in Figure 5.2 below.

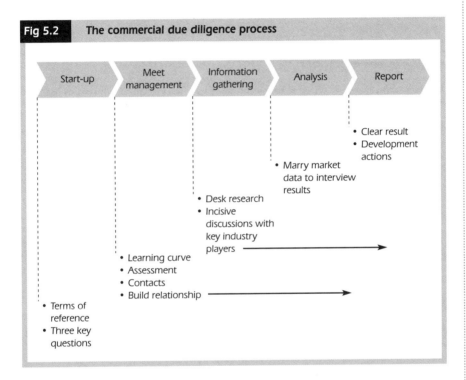

Fig 5.2   The commercial due diligence process

As can be seen, it is a five stage process, each stage outlined in the next section.

Start-up

Like all due diligence, CDD should not be conducted in a vacuum. The CDD team must be aware of the full circumstances of the deal, why it is being done, how it fits with the buyer's strategy and what the buyers intend to do with it once the deal is done. Only then can the CDD team do its job properly and add value.

Tempting though it might be to go for full value for money and draft terms of reference that address every last commercial issue, this is usually counter-productive. By the time you get to the presentation you will realise that there are a small number of issues critical to the target's future. If the CDD team has done only what it was told (and inexperienced ones will) it will not have addressed the key issues facing the business. Prioritisation is therefore essential so that CDD focuses on areas of uncertainty, risk and upside. Some examples might be:

Uncertainty

- The market is set to accept this technology and take off, but will users commit now, having already hesitated for a number of years?
- The target has a subsidiary in an unrelated business area, which we would like to dispose of, but we do not know how marketable it is and we cannot afford to be left with an unattractive, unsaleable, asset

Risk

- The business is more profitable than all of its competitors, yet it has no structural reason to be so. How can we be sure that this is sustainable?
- Much of the success of the business depends on the successful launch of a new version of its most important product. Will the product launch achieve what management claim?

Upside

- The business is less profitable than its competitors, we want to improve margins, but is this achievable?
- The US market is ripe for exploitation and it will just take a national distribution deal to achieve penetration. How realistic is this?

Meet management

It is best to meet the management of the target company at the start of the CDD programme. The aim of this is to:

- Reassure them that the CDD team is highly experienced, appreciates the sensitivities involved, and will not disrupt the business' current commercial relationships. Think how apprehensive you would feel about a bunch of consultants interviewing your best customers even without the added risk that they might let slip that you are selling out
- Obtain a thorough briefing on the business and the market
- Sell the benefits of the work. CDD is not just a tyre-kicking exercise. It should collect valuable market intelligence and there should always be a PR spin-off with customers
- Agree the best way for the CDD team to approach customers, and other industry contacts
- Agree the internal contacts with whom the CDD team should be in touch. After the meeting with top management the CDD team needs to know who in the management team is aware of the transaction. Although the focus of CDD is primarily external, the CDD team may want to interview some of these key

managers in the initial project phase such as managing directors of subsidiaries and senior customer facing managers

- Obtain contact details for customers and others who are familiar with the business
- Open channels of communication so that important topics can be discussed or validated as the work proceeds

Mid-deal management meetings can be delicate. It is best to take experienced people. Some consultancies make the mistake of sending in bright but young consultants who rub management up the wrong way. This is a very sensitive time for management. There is a lot at stake including their livelihoods and, for owner-managers, their retirement plans. On top of this is the inherent stress and disruption of the due diligence process itself. If the CDD team fails to build a positive relationship at this point it will struggle to do its work effectively.

Disclosure and confidentiality

A major element of CDD is customer and other interviews. Rarely can a CDD team tell the whole truth when explaining the reasons for its enquiries to people outside the business, therefore a key matter to establish with management is the extent to which customer and other interviews can be conducted on a disclosed basis. The closer to the truth the better. The best compromise is for the target to agree that the CDD team can say it is conducting a strategic review or customer care programme on its behalf. This platform requires the full cooperation of the target's management and it must fit in with the company's customer relationship programme. One target once refused to go along with a customer care platform with the curious boast that it never carries out customer surveys and its customers would know that. As might be expected with such an enlightened target company involved, that particular deal did not go ahead.

If customers are to be interviewed on behalf of the target company, staff need to be made aware of the research programme otherwise there can be embarrassment and confusion.

Management may offer to hand over existing customer surveys. Few companies conduct customer care surveys which approach the level of professionalism and detail which a well run CDD programme involves, so prior surveys are almost invariably of little practical use.

A customer care platform is not going to work with competitors. Competitor interviews need particularly skilled interviewers 'doing some work on the market' or 'doing some work on behalf of a potential investor'.

The vendor, or the financial adviser running the transaction, can influence the process and attempt to limit the number of discussions which are held. It is perfectly reasonable for a vendor to wish to protect confidentiality and to understand the nature of the discussions. It is in the acquirer's own interest to avoid unhelpful rumours in the market which could destabilise relationships between the company and its customers. What is not reasonable is for the vendor to seek to prevent the acquirer from talking on a confidential or undisclosed basis to the people who know the real strengths and weaknesses of the company. The seller who seeks to prevent reasonable access to important sources of information such as customers runs the risk of appearing to hide unpleasant facts, which is usually counter-productive because a skilled CDD team can, if necessary, make the enquiries without the target knowing. Similarly, the target sending someone to listen in to telephone interviews is to be resisted. It is highly disruptive because it limits the free exchange between interviewer and interviewee.

Selection of interview targets

The CDD team is to some extent reliant on management to advise which interviewees will yield the best information and provide contact details. Some management teams are tempted to hand-pick customers while keeping the CDD team away from problem cases. A good CDD programme will not rely totally on management contacts.

Management may be wary of some of the other contacts which the CDD team will want to speak to. There may be sensitivity over suppliers if contracts are currently being negotiated. Former employees can be a particularly sensitive area; they are mentally ostracised as part of a natural management defence mechanism. The trick is to see through this and go with your instincts. Ideally the entire interview programme, including competitor interviews should be agreed with management. However the CDD team should not accept being spoon-fed. It should make its own decisions about who it contacts whilst ensuring that it does not conduct any interviews which disrupt the business.

Information gathering

There are three sources for information in a commercial due diligence programme:

- External published information (also known as secondary)
- External unpublished information (also known as primary)
- Internal information

External published information (secondary sources)

'Secondary' in this context means published, or publicly available.

The detailed research phase starts with a desk research exercise, reviewing all relevant published, or secondary sources. A substantial volume of information is easily available from public sources and through commercial databases.

Consultancies conducting CDD may also already have relevant data on the target markets.

Secondary sources are invaluable as a precursor to investigations in the market, using primary sources. They provide basic data and they can give the commercial due diligence team valuable background information about the industry. Industry participants are generally happy to talk to people if they understand the issues. They will soon get bored and lose patience if they need to explain the basics of their industry in order for the conversation to continue.

The desk research continues throughout the project. As the issues develop, the desk research becomes increasingly focused. With so much information available through public sources, desk researchers run the risk of picking up useful information, but not the best information. Using less than the best information obviously reduces the quality of the subsequent analysis. Instead of just going online, you should develop a desk research strategy.

Some basics for designing desk research strategies are:

- Integrate desk research with the overall research design
- Know what you need to be looking for and why you need it – how does it fit with the bigger picture? How are you going to use it when you get it?
- Know what sources are available and develop a checklist of information sources to use
- Develop keywords to assist in online searches

Information comes from three main sources:

- Commercial databases which publish their own or aggregate other people's information
- Public libraries where a wide range of materials in addition to commercial databases are available and staff can he helpful
- The Internet which can yield less structured, but still valuable, information

Secondary sources have their limitations. They are general rather than specific. They cover large, mass markets but refer to niches only in passing and are rarely completely up-to-date, which is why CDD relies heavily on primary sources.

External unpublished information (primary sources)

The core of a commercial due diligence programme is detailed discussions with customers, distributors, regulators, competitors, industry observers, and other relevant contacts in the market. Even in very well documented industries, such as telecoms and financial services, these interviews remain essential. The industry's reputable published statistical reports should be exploited to the full but it is not possible to segment the market or analyse key purchase criteria without speaking to market participants.

Figure 5.3 below shows a generic list of the various primary information sources which a CDD team typically considers calling.

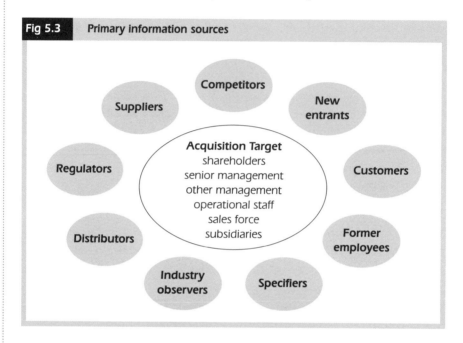

Fig 5.3   **Primary information sources**

Customers pay the bills, making their opinions the most important. They are best grouped into three categories:

- current
- former, and
- non/lost

An excellent customer fit is always a good start point for an acquisition. This is not just so that the buyer can cross sell, but it also means that the buyer understands how to deal with that group of customers. It is therefore unsurprising that early forms of commercial due diligence were in fact enhanced customer referencing exercises.

If customers hold a business in high esteem and will continue to buy from it, then its future is more likely to be healthy than if the opposite applies. However, customers are customers for a reason, therefore the scope of interviews needs to be widened to overcome their in-built bias. Non-customers are part of this widening.

Distributors, wholesalers, resellers, retailers or whoever else sells the product are almost as important as the end customers themselves. In some markets these distributors are the company's direct customers. They are almost inevitably better-informed than the end users about the detailed workings of the target company and the strengths and weaknesses of its products.

Sometimes the relationship between principal and distributor is not straightforward. For example, a leading French financial services company sold half its products through one nationally-organised distributor. Enquiries revealed that this distributor strongly objected to certain conditions of its seven-year contract with the principal. These conditions had been acceptable at the start of the contract period, but had been made obsolete by changes in the industry. The principal obstinately refused to amend the terms of the contract and the distributor was actively planning to move on once the contract came to an end in less than a year's time. This would wipe out half of the principal's sales.

Specifiers can be as influential as customers and distributors in certain businesses, most notably in the construction industry. If the architect has specified a product 'or equivalent' then there is a strong chance that the builder will use it. Doctors are specifiers of pharmaceuticals and care homes. IT consultants specify computer hardware and software. Teachers specify school books.

Regulators can have a profound impact on industries, often in ways which are quite unforeseen. When the UK government started to encourage employees to make personal arrangements for their pensions it did not expect the pensions industry to adopt the forcible selling techniques which have given their sector a bad name.

The box below sets out examples of CDD programmes where regulatory change was a key consideration:

- The target company was launching an alternative directory enquiries service in various European countries. Deregulation of directory enquiries across Europe may well open up opportunities for new service providers, but delays in implementation and the ability of incumbents to slow liberalisation can delay their entry. In such cases, new entrants recoup their substantial set-up costs more slowly and their well-worked business plans are rendered invalid.

- The target company manufactured a particular kind of safe. The UK regulations require this kind of safe to withstand attack by a thermal lance for a period of 15 seconds. The equivalent German regulations require that it withstand the attentions of a tank! As with many industries, the European Commission had the unenviable task of 'harmonising' these ▶

83

> very different requirements, and in CDD it was important to ascertain the likely direction of future legislation. By talking to the relevant EC Directorate as well as numerous well-informed industry sources it became clear that the more rigorous German standards would not be imposed across the board.
>
> - The target company made spare parts for lorries. The parts were 'generic', in that they met the same technical and performance specifications as the original parts, but they were not made or badged by the Original Equipment Maker (OEM). An important part of the rationale for the deal was the possibility of exporting the company's products to other European countries, and this meant understanding the current and likely future attitude of continental European regulators towards such 'copy' parts for vehicles.

Suppliers can be an excellent source of information, particularly when the supplier sees the acquisition target as a key account. If you want to buy a Ford dealership then it would be a good idea to find out what Ford thinks of the business and its prospects. If you are buying a cable maker – or any other capital-intensive manufacturer – then it is worth interviewing the major equipment suppliers. They should know their target customers well. They may even be able to benchmark the target's capex programme or manufacturing efficiency against its competitors. Suppliers are normally hungry for more information on their target markets and keen to identify new angles into customers which makes them willing to talk to outsiders.

Competitors usually keep a close eye on each other, they should have the most carefully researched information about the market and its future prospects – and if they are doing their job properly, they should have studied the weaknesses of the target company. Asked in the right way, competitors will usually be happy to talk about their rivals' weaknesses to anyone who listens. An ideal question to ask a competitor might be: '...so, given your comments, if you were running xyz (target company) what would you do?'

Former employees can be an excellent source of information, but they are not always easy to include in the research programme. First, they can be hard to find. Once found, their opinions sometimes have to be discounted as they can have personal reasons for liking or disliking their former employer and former colleagues, particularly if they left under difficult circumstances. But they can also be superb sources of information. For example the customers of a market-leading instrumentation company unanimously agreed that the target company had the best products in its market, thanks to a first-class R&D department. Speaking to R&D people in the main competitor it was apparent that they were recent recruits from the target. It transpired that the target company's management had emasculated the R&D department in order to improve the results of a disappointing year. The move was effective in the short term, but in the long term the company would clearly suffer from a lack of new products in an increasingly competitive market.

New entrants to a market will usually carry out a considerable amount of independent research before taking a market entry decision, so their views and plans are normally worth listening to. These companies can be hard to identify, although most market moves are advertised in some way; for example, in technical markets the research community will often get wind of potential developments.

Industry observers such as trade journalists, trade association officials, academics, and consultants follow developments in their industries closely, and are familiar with many of the major players. Talking to them should provide a good introductory briefing to an industry and its issues. Industry observers can also refer you to other useful contacts. The downside is that industry observers have their own agendas, like trying to pick up CDD work for themselves.

Trade journalists are often talkative and are delighted to share their views with interested outsiders. Generally the more niche the industry, the more accessible and talkative they are. Trade associations have to be careful to avoid being seen to promote the interests of one member firm above others, so they are rarely willing to offer opinions about individual companies. Nonetheless they can often help to describe some of the key characteristics of the industry, which helps to inform later discussions.

Conducting the interviews

The more people that are interviewed, the safer it is to draw conclusions. But CDD is not mass market research, where sample size is all-important, and there is a limit to how many people can be contacted. The number of interviews is determined by the:

- Number of markets served
- Number of customers
- Level of uncertainty
- Level of risk
- Quality of published data

The initial issue analysis should have identified those sectors or territories which are either critical to the future performance of the whole business, or which are producing troubling results and require detailed investigation.

Personal meetings usually generate more information and insights than telephone discussions, but they take up far more time. Arranging a meeting with, say, a marketing director of a drug company can take as much time as actually holding a detailed phone conversation with a less junior manager or less pressured person in an industry less concerned about confidentiality. In most cases face-to-face meetings are only worth the time and effort if the customer concerned accounts for a substantial proportion of sales.

An essential skill is getting people to talk. The secrets of success include:

- Using a referral or introduction, for example:
  - 'Company X (the target) has asked to review its service levels and run a customer care programme.'
  - 'Fred at the trade association said that you are the best person to talk to about this.'
  - 'We have included [all the major industry players] in our survey and would not like your organisation to be left out.'
- Being pleasant, interesting and persuasive to charm the respondents into submission
- Appeal to egos. When people with interesting jobs talk about their jobs they are in effect talking about themselves, often their favourite subject
- Allowing people to think. Respondents benefit from explaining a process or a situation to intelligent, encouraging listeners, as it forces them to get their own thoughts on the subject in order. They enjoy a conversation in which they are doing most of the talking, not because of rampant egomania, but because they are reviewing their own ideas as they go along
- Giving something in return. Experienced consultants can make some observations which even the most experienced (and most cynical) market participant will find valuable. Good CDD interviews are a two-way street, not simply a process of sucking information from unwitting victims

Do people tell the truth?

As if doing CDD is not difficult enough already, the people contacted can sometimes mislead you. They rarely tell straightforward lies, but they often fail to tell the truth. Sometimes people:

- Do not remember, or they mis-remember certain important facts
- Misinterpret or misunderstand the question and provide the answer to another question – for example they provide the market size for all apples as opposed to just green apples

- Never knew the detail in the first place, but would be embarrassed to appear less knowledgeable than they think they should be and so they provide a well-intentioned, but misleading answer
- Withhold information because they are uncertain how it will be used

Experienced interviewers think on their feet and spot erroneous or incoherent information and then find a sympathetic way in which to challenge it.

Internal information

CDD should not rely solely on information provided by the company, or internal information held by the acquirer. Nonetheless, internal information is required to understand the business and allow external comparisons. The commercial due diligence team will normally request the business plan, performance measures and market-related information.

The target's business or strategic plan is a key document for the acquirer to obtain and validate. It is the job of the CDD team to validate its projections and the assumptions which lie behind it. Often the forecasts may have been re-worked and re-presented by the seller's corporate finance house, in an information memorandum (IM). An IM is a sales document, which inevitably presents the business in the best possible light. Watch out for unsubstantiated claims, 3D graphics and graphs which do not begin at zero.

Management should be able to provide performance measures on the business. Key Performance Indicators (KPIs) are hard measures, although not typically based on financial information.

Examples of KPIs include:

- Hotel occupancy rates
- Production 'up time'
- Product reject rate
- Consultant/service employee utilisation ratios
- Sales conversion ratios
- Average revenue per customer
- Customer retention rates
- Advertising page yield

Whilst an internal analysis of the KPIs, across a division or from one year to another, is useful, the real value comes from competitor benchmarking. This requires careful planning and advanced interview skills to ensure that the information obtained from competitors can be used for valid comparisons.

Market information

The CDD team should ask management to share relevant market information which the company holds. Reports and documents to ask for include:

- Market reports
- Customer surveys
- Customer lists
- Development papers
- Trade magazines
- Trade show catalogues

This information is a good starting point, but that is all. Management teams rarely quantify and segment their market accurately. If the company has sales of $50 m and the market is supposedly worth $1 bn you can be fairly sure that its addressable segment will be much less that the $1 bn figure taken from a market report.

Reporting

At the end of a commercial due diligence exercise you will get a report. As mentioned above, you should insist on a presentation because words on a page never tell the whole story. Besides, a due diligence report, based on the same facts, can sound optimistic or pessimistic depending on the author.

The reporting topics and style differ according to the transaction, who is doing the work and most importantly, the audience. Commercial due diligence exercises are allowed no more than four or five weeks – and often less. Because time is short, it is essential to focus on the critical issues which means concentrating on the areas of least information and greatest risk.

The vendor will not be privy to the report in the first instance but as a part of the negotiations the buyer may choose to release part or even all the report to the vendor as a tactic to prove that the business has less value than originally thought.

Table 5.2 is a CDD report format which has stood the test of time and has proved highly satisfactory for a wide variety of acquirers and investors.

Table 5.2	A CDD report format

Report section	Explanation
Contents	
Terms of reference	The brief and the methodology used to fulfil it
The answer on a page	A single page of bullet points, summarising all of the key issues
Conclusions	Conclusions for each of the individual markets, business units and revenue streams analysed
Executive summary (optional)	A formal written explanation of the 'answer' and conclusions
Analysis	Structured analysis of all of the issues which have culminated in the conclusions. The analysis should be based on factual information. When facts are not available, opinions should be used, so long as they can be substantiated
Supporting data	Records of all important discussions, and profiles of key players in the market
Appendices	Background explanatory material about the company and its industry

Analysis

CDD has a number of similarities to a standard strategy review or the type of strategic marketing review which would be carried out prior to launching a new product, it therefore uses a number of the techniques and tools used in such reviews.

SWOT analysis

A well considered SWOT, a review of the company's Strengths, Weaknesses, Opportunities and Threats, is very valuable. Unfortunately SWOTs are often quickly and poorly put together, thereby devaluing them.

Like other tools, a SWOT analysis is an aid to thought, so it is dangerous to be too prescriptive about it. In general, however, the Strengths and Weaknesses are internal to the company (i.e. concerned with its people, abilities and products), and are apparent today. The Threats and Opportunities are external (i.e. to do with the market and the competition) and to do with the future. Figure 5.4 shows the SWOT of a business known as Father Christmas plc.

Fig 5.4	SWOT analysis: Father Christmas plc

Strengths	Weaknesses
• Distribution • Brand • etc	• Scepticism amongst over-fives • Seasonal sales cycle • etc
Opportunities	**Threats**
• Theme parks • Easter • etc	• Religious decline • etc

Key purchase criteria

Customers evaluate suppliers before purchasing, but it is not always clear to suppliers what their customers' key purchase criteria are. Customer requirements may also vary from market segment to market segment, and even from customer to customer. This underlines the importance of segmenting the market accurately, as well as understanding precise customer needs.

Table 5.3 below shows that some customers of removal firms think mainly about price, and if the odd book or piece of cutlery is lost or damaged that is less important than the money saved. For other customers the critical thing is that every possession arrives intact and price is a lesser concern. For others again, the process of moving is so stressful that the most important part of the service is simply the quality of service – the courtesy and the apparent concern for a smooth operation.

Table 5.3	Different key purchase criteria amongst customers of removals firms

Customer type	Key purchase criterion
Price-driven	Lowest price
Possession-driven	Avoidance of damage or loss
Stress-driven	Evident concern and consideration

Critical success factors

Critical success factors (CSFs) define what a company must get right to achieve its goals and fulfil its strategy. The CSFs for a sports car company would include R&D, engineering excellence and branding. These deliver the performance and reputation required by the customer. Similarly the CSFs for the family car company would include wide distribution, quality management and marketing in order to deliver price, reliability and resale value.

Table 5.4 shows the links between key purchase criteria and critical success factors, and how they then can be measured by Key Performance Indicators (KPIs).

Table 5.4 **Relationship between KPCs, CSFs and KPIs in the bicycle market**

Segment	Low end	Mid-range	Premium
Key purchase criteria	1. Price 2. Availability 3. Fashionable	1. Quality 2. Brand 3. Price	1. Performance 2. Design/innovation 3. Brand
Strategy (Value propositions)	Low-end bikes sold through department and discount stores under retailer's own brand	Medium-price bikes sold primarily through specialist retailers under manufacturer's brand	High-price bikes for enthusiasts
Critical success factors	• Global sourcing and low wage assembly • Supply contracts with major retailers • Supply chain efficiency	• Cost efficiency • Reputation for quality • Distribution	• Quality of components and assembly • Innovative design • Reputation and brand management
Key performance indicators	• Cost per unit • Growth in number of outlets • Average inventory level	• Cost per unit • Percentage of returns • Time to order	• Percentage of defective bikes • Customer satisfaction rating • Brand awareness level

Forecast analysis

A critical element of CDD is to provide a clear opinion on the target company's forecasts and their achievability. The simple way to analyse forecasts is to establish growth in the relevant market segments and then to review the variance between the target's forecast growth rate and that of the market (see Figure 5.5). Plenty of companies claim to serve markets which are growing at 3–4 per cent p.a., yet their sales forecast is for 6–8 per cent p.a. This means that the company is gaining market share. Before buying it, you must work out if it really is capable of gaining share and who in particular is losing share. This is where a critical success factor (CSF) analysis can bridge any gaps. If the business can be proven to have an above-average performance against CSFs for the industry, then it can be expected to outperform the market. Conversely if it is below average on its CSF performance then any claim to outperform the market is difficult to believe.

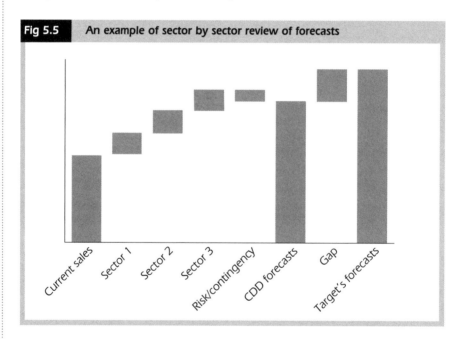

Fig 5.5 An example of sector by sector review of forecasts

Business models and cultures

Business models and cultures in similar businesses vary, particularly between different countries. We can all describe the differences between British Airways, Virgin Atlantic and Ryanair. The informal, even colloquial, expressions we use are the tools that people will need if they are to attempt to integrate two or more cultures.

Do not forget that a company's business model will reflect its culture, and vice versa. Culturally you cannot just swap the employees of BA, Virgin and Ryanair. Each airline would get even more complaints!

The important points are to:

- Understand the business model so that integration actions do not damage the business
- Assess the impact of any cultural differences on the integration process

Who does commercial due diligence?

Commercial due diligence can be carried out internally or by an external organisation. Some frequent acquirers have built teams and developed a great of deal of in-house CDD expertise. If you have the resource, conducting CDD in-house saves money, builds expertise and, most importantly, avoids any loss of information between the CDD and the acquisition integration phase. However, most acquirers do not have sufficient resources with the right skills and experience to cope with the intense workload of an acquisition. Moreover, an in-house team cannot disguise its identity and will find it difficult to talk to market participants, especially competitors. The other problem with in-house CDD teams is 'going native' and saying 'yes' to a bad deal. The situation can become impossibly uncomfortable for staff members if a senior director is on the warpath and wants to push his pet project through.

A range of external firms offer CDD services. The major audit firms have set out their stalls with some form of CDD offering, although the quality of their results can be impeded by their fear of litigation. The mainstream management consultancies are perhaps too well qualified for the work and are often expensive. Other marketing consultancies can suffer from the inverse problem. Acquirers are therefore typically best off using a specialist CDD consultancy.

Case study 5.1 Ferranti

In 1988 Ferranti bought International Signal Controls (ISC) without conducting CDD, and bankrupted itself. Ferranti was a long-established British electronics company with particular expertise in the defence sector. ISC was an American defence electronics company which claimed to have won a series of lucrative contracts with the defence procurement bodies of a range of foreign governments.

It took some time for the fact that several of these contracts did not in fact exist to be discovered, and it was two years before the resultant gaping hole in Ferranti's balance sheet finally sank the company. Parts of the company survive within former competitors like Marconi and Thales. How could this disaster happen, and why did it take so long for the consequences to follow?

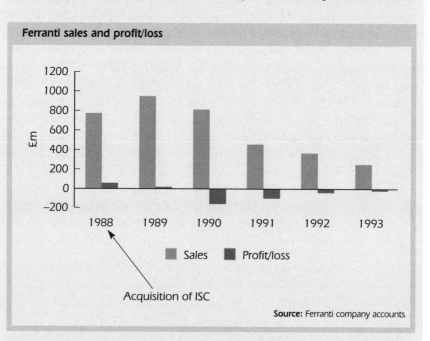

Ferranti sales and profit/loss

Source: Ferranti company accounts

One reason why Ferranti bought ISC was to defend itself against a likely hostile bid from another British group, STC. Ferranti knew that STC had looked at ISC itself but had decided against going ahead. Ferranti believed that acquiring ISC would create a sort of poison pill, and thus divert STC's attentions. It was correct, but the pill was more poisonous than expected.

▶

ISC persuaded Ferranti that certain contracts were too sensitive to be investigated, and that following the acquisition they would need to be 'ring-fenced' and run separately from the main business. Ferranti, in a hurry to close the deal before STC's bid materialised, agreed.

Amazingly, none of the claimed customers was approached to confirm the existence of the contracts. Admittedly, the nature of the business made such contacts more difficult than is usually the case – and one of the most important contacts had the misfortune to make an unplanned exit from a helicopter in mid-flight. But these obstacles do not diminish the need for proper commercial due diligence. The financial due diligence was also sloppy as Ferranti relied on the audit, but it was the failure to carry out commercial due diligence that sank the ship.

Conclusion

Commercial due diligence is the process of investigating a company and its markets. It employs information from the target company and secondary sources including published market information, but it also relies heavily on primary sources – customers, competitors and other market participants. The key skills required include the ability to conduct these interviews effectively, the ability to analyse the industry and the ability to tie all the information to the company's competitive position and to its business plan. Commercial due diligence is one of the most powerful ways to reduce the risk in a transaction: it should also help you negotiate the best deal, and plan post-acquisition integration actions.

As already noted, there is usually a close relationship between commercial and financial due diligence. Indeed it may sometimes appear that a financial due diligence report covers most of the commercial issues. In fact commercial and financial due diligence are quite different processes, although they do indeed seek to answer some of the same questions. The critical difference is that a commercial due diligence investigation is based primarily on information available outside the target company, while a financial due diligence investigation is based primarily on documents obtained from the target and on interviews with its management. The commercial and financial investigations therefore complement each other in arriving at the ultimate goal, which is a view on the likely future performance of the target business.

Financial investigations

What are the key issues to be covered?

Financial due diligence (FDD) is not an audit. FDD should at all times be focused on the future. It frequently draws on historical information, but examining past events is useful only if it provides an insight into the future. Thus financial due diligence is about identifying the target company's maintainable earnings and assessing the degree of risk attached to them.

The key financial issues covered by FDD are usually:

- Earnings
- Assets
- Liabilities
- Cash flows
- Net cash or debt, and
- Management

Earnings

FDD should assess the level of maintainable earnings of the target business because it usually provides a guide to the future performance of the business. This requires a thorough understanding of the entire business and its market: it is much more than the identification and stripping-out of non-recurring profit and loss items.

Assets

FDD should review the business's assets. Again, this work will have an eye on the future – it will look at accounting issues, but it should be mostly concerned with the nature of the assets, and their suitability for the business. Cash flow is going to suffer if assets are reaching the end of their life and will need replacing soon after the business is yours. FDD can also identify any assets the business owns, but does not necessarily need.

The investigation can also compare the market value of assets with their net book value. For example, low net book values may give a misleading view of the level of capital required by the business over the long term, and so may flatter the true maintainable earnings of the business. FDD should consider asset ownership; a sale and leaseback transaction may be an efficient way to release cash, indirectly helping to finance the acquisition itself.

Liabilities

The investigation of liabilities should look for any liabilities which have not been disclosed, or whose value has been underestimated. This part of the investigation tends to be more backward-looking: but, of course, the key underlying objective is to spot any unexpected future costs. Under-funded pension liabilities would be an obvious example.

Cash flows

To what extent are profits not reflected as net cash inflows? There may be good reasons for a business not to generate cash – the business may have invested heavily, or a business may be growing rapidly with the increased working capital requirement draining cash. These are important issues for any new owner of a business who may have to find extra cash to finance it properly.

Net cash or debt

Businesses are typically valued free of cash or debt; if either is in the company, this may impact on the transaction price. Assessing the level of cash or debt is not always easy. If the business is very seasonal – such as tourism or retail – or if some financial debt instruments are accounted for off balance sheet the calculations are harder to make.

Management

An FDD team will have a lot of contact, discussion and interviews with the target's management. Consequently a commercially minded FDD team should be well placed to comment on the strengths, weaknesses and even organisation of the management team. Experienced acquirers ask for these opinions as they are keen to anticipate how the target's management team will fit into the new environment of the combined businesses.

Where does the information come from?

The investigating accountant will obtain information from a wide variety of sources, but almost always the sources of information will be inside the target company.

Shopping lists

It is common practice to provide the vendors and their advisers with a detailed information request list (or 'shopping list'). FDD advisers have standard lists. The experienced ones know that it is best to tailor them to the circumstances of each particular transaction. Too many due diligence investigations get off to a bad start because the various advisers inundate the unsuspecting vendors with huge ill-considered requests for information, with considerable duplication across the different lists. Understandably, the vendors take this badly. Then either because they are genuinely annoyed or for tactical reasons, they may exploit this poor preparation to put the purchaser on the back foot, trying to weaken his negotiating position.

Appendix A provides an example of a shortened FDD information request list.

Interviews with the target's management

Interviews form a critical part of most financial investigations. They will often be based around documents, but the investigating accountant will also steer the conversation away from hard issues, always seeking to improve his under-standing of the target business, its strengths and weaknesses, what it can achieve and where it might prove vulnerable. Covering similar ground with several different members of the target's management team can be enlightening; for example, comparing the views of the managing director, finance director and production director.

As the sale of a business is often a traumatic period filled with uncertainty for its managers, the investigating accountant must be sensitive to the different circumstances of each transaction and each manager's agenda. A newly-recruited manager may have little 'baggage' and be more ready to criticise the business while a long-standing manager has valuable, detailed knowledge but may be less objective and feel that any criticism of the business amounts to a criticism of him personally.

An owner manager, who has spent his life building his business, will natu-rally tend to present his business in a favourable light. The prospects of a pro-fessional manager who is not a vendor and who is being 'sold with the business' are quite different; he may quite quickly 'change sides' and identify with the purchaser, his prospective employer. He or she may even be motivated to show the business in a poor light, so that good performance following the acquisition is attributed to his subsequent good management.

The target's historical advisers

It is common practice for the investigating accountants to review the working papers of the auditors to the target, and to interview the auditors. This is for two reasons:

- To gain an initial understanding of the target company and its business
- To get a feel for the quality of the audit, and so gain comfort that any clean audit opinions are supported by appropriate audit work

But the target must formally give the auditors permission to open their files and the auditors will usually seek a 'hold harmless' letter signed by the investigating accountants and their client to ensure they cannot be sued. Negotiating this and related letters can be painfully slow and even then the auditors may not open up their files quickly. Sometimes no agreement is reached at all, forcing the purchaser and its advisers to manage somehow, perhaps by extending the scope of their investigations. In a similar vein, it is also useful for the investigating accountants to exchange views with the tax and legal advisers of the target, so long as access problems can be overcome.

What are the contents of an FDD report?

The contents of a typical FDD investigation are:

- History and commercial activities
- Organisational structure and employees
- Information systems
- Accounting policies
- Sales, cost of sales, gross margins
- Cash flow
- Net assets
- Taxation
- Financial issues relating to pension schemes
- Financial projections

Each of these is examined in turn below:

History and commercial activities

The prime purpose of FDD is to assess the level of maintainable earnings of the target. The underlying objective in reviewing any historical information is to give an insight into the potential of the business to generate profits.

Examples of issues which might arise in the investigation of a target's history and commercial activities include:

- *Previous changes in the shareholders*. This may be benign, but could, for example, indicate that the founders fell out and perhaps the remaining shareholders are difficult to live with
- *Changes in the management*. The recent loss of a key manager may cause immediate difficulties to the business, but may also say something about the business or its market. Why was the target unable to retain a key manager?

Perhaps there was a disagreement on strategy, or the manager believed that the company would soon be in decline. Ex-managers may make useful interviewees for the commercial due diligence team

- *Insufficient investment because the company was being groomed for sale*. Reducing levels of investment will flatter profits by reducing the depreciation charge and enhancing cash flows at the expense of the future profitability of the business, but this is not sustainable over a long period. The new owners might be forced to spend to catch up

- *Dependence on a few suppliers*. This may make the business vulnerable

- *Dependence on a few customers*. Such dependence exposes the business to risk. It is important to understand why it is dependent on a few customers, and whether it can decrease this dependence

- *Cyclicality and seasonality*. If different to the acquirer's experience this may lead to some unwelcome surprises if poorly understood. Buying at the top of the cycle may involve paying too much

- *Competitive threats*. This could be due, for example, to entry by a new competitor or from emerging technology

- *Disputes with a major supplier*. These may be revealed through interviews or through observing that payments to that supplier are behind or that the target has changed to another supplier

- *Problems of quality control*. Quality problems may be revealed by a high level of credit notes, reflecting numerous returns; or by a review of credit control – slow-paying customers may not be happy

Organisational structure and employees

Legal due diligence focuses on the contractual relationships with management and employees. FDD should assess whether the people can drive the business forward after the acquisition. Investigating accountants will be interested in:

- A *high degree of dependence on a few managers*. This may require the buyer to take steps to tie such employees into the business or it may trigger a search for a suitable successor. Significant weaknesses in the management team can arise in both owner-managed and corporate businesses

- *Culture*. A culture very different from that of the acquirer often leads to a subsequent clash of cultures, which may be harmful and difficult to manage. Marks & Spencer never really got to grips with Brooks Brothers

- *Duplication*. Duplication with the acquirer's management team should be an opportunity, but the acquirer must plan for how any such duplication will be quickly dealt with following completion of the transaction. The Travellers/ Citicorp merger was a disaster due to a high level of overlap and 'job-sharing'

FDD can also reveal a range of issues in relation to the employees:

- *Use of overtime.* The target may make extensive use of overtime work, which may not be sustainable in the long term. British Airways had to cancel flights when its check-in staff would not work overtime, even at attractive rates of pay

- *A shortage of suitable skilled workers.* This could restrict the potential for growth

- *A strongly unionised workforce.* The workforce may be strongly unionised, making the reaction of the unions to a change in ownership a key factor to manage. Ford struggled with the unions at Jaguar. What you must also be careful to avoid is introducing unionisation into your own plants as a result of the acquisition

- *A high level of staff turnover.* There may be a high level of staff turnover reflecting other weaknesses in the business

- *Rates of pay and other employment conditions.* Rates of pay or other conditions of employment in the target may be significantly different from those of the acquirer. It may be difficult to resist pressure to bring all staff up to a similar remuneration package, so increasing the cost base of the combined business. British Airways suffered from this problem, for example, when it acquired Dan Air

- *The ease with which headcount reductions can be made.* Redundancies may be hard to make, due to the shape of the organisation, associated costs or procedures. It cost United Technologies tens of millions of dollars to close its Paris office

Information systems

FDD of a company with weak information systems is likely to prove difficult, may overshoot deadlines and is more expensive than the investigation of a company with strong systems. Strong information systems also give confidence in the business as a whole; it is properly managed in accordance with carefully-drawn-up plans.

Accounting policies

The review of accounting policies is an important part of FDD, even where the overall scope is limited. The reported profits of a business can depend very significantly on its accounting policies and the interpretation of them. The investigating accountant should examine carefully any changes to accounting policies. Although less easy to do, it should also look at their application.

The problem is amplified across borders: different countries adopt different accounting practices, leading to significant differences in reported results. The definition of financial debt is critical as it can have a simple and direct effect on the price payable for a target where the price is negotiated free of cash and of financial debt.

Some examples of issues that can arise on the review of accounting policies and information systems include:

- *Income recognition*. The approach to the recognition of income on long-term contracts can vary even when companies apparently have similar accounting policies

- *Depreciation rates*. Depreciation rates for similar assets may vary significantly from company to company

- *Provisions*. Provisions against investments, including goodwill, can vary enormously as they can against contingent liabilities, slow-moving or obsolete stocks and slow-paying trade debtors. All are subjective and may be used to flatter profits

- *Stock valuation*. Stock valuation is always the subject of debate, particularly in manufacturing businesses, as final stock valuations impact declared profits

Sales, cost of sales, gross margins

Much of the value of a business lies in its capacity to generate gross margins. FDD will identify and strip out any non-recurring events and profits to establish the main underlying trends in the performance of the business.

One FDD enquiry into a retailer of domestic appliances noted a steady trend in gross margin. The retailer's gross margins were highly dependent on the price it paid for stock, which in turn made them highly dependent on the rebates it received from suppliers. These were volume-dependent and only applied if the retailer bought more than a specified amount. Volume rebates were awarded in January, based on the retailer's purchases in the previous twelve months. The retailer's year end was September and therefore it had to accrue for any rebates in its management accounts. The management accounts and current year forecast contained no accrual for volume rebates – so how come gross margin was steady? FDD revealed that the rebates had been taken at the product level which was not only the wrong accounting treatment but was also highly misleading because this year's purchases were not going to be big enough to justify a rebate.

The review of overheads is typically easier; it will involve explaining variations from year to year and, in particular, will seek to identify any exceptional items as well as any ongoing changes to the overhead base. This leads to a view on what the likely level of the overhead might be in the future.

The FDD team can draw on many sources of information to review trading results. Typically it will begin with statutory and management accounting information. It will also be particularly interested in unofficial information, which is used by the target's management to monitor and control the business – something not always included in the management accounts. This can contribute significantly to understanding the business: of course it also implies that the management and control systems can be improved.

Cash flow

The FDD team then needs to understand the relationship between accounting profits and cash generation. A persistent failure to generate cash while continuing to show accounting profits might suggest that the profits and the underlying accounting treatment are questionable – the profits may not be real.

The review should also analyse the quality of treasury management. Is the business financed efficiently? Does management fully understand cash flows, predicting and managing the cash position?

Net assets

We have already made the point that an FDD investigation of assets and liabilities is not an audit of assets and liabilities. An audit checks their existence and values them, generally based on historical cost. The assets and liabilities of a business are of interest to FDD only insofar as they contribute to the future earnings potential of the business.

Nonetheless, the review of assets can call on the accounting records as the starting point for enquiries. FDD should assess whether the business has the right assets of the right quality, and is able to handle current and forecast volumes of business. Is there an urgent need to make substantial investments in new equipment? Or are there assets, perfectly valid from an accounting and audit point of view, but which are not relevant to the core business and which can be sold?

The review of liabilities can also begin with the accounting records, but the primary concern may well be with those that do not figure in the accounting records. An experienced investigator should have a good idea of how to look for them in interviews, and especially in interviews with employees far from finance (production or sales, for example).

Examples of issues which might arise on a review of a company's assets and liabilities are as follows:

- *Creative financing.* A company might own the freehold of its main premises, allowing the acquirer to consider a sale and leaseback agreement which would release cash

- *Outdated production equipment and systems.* Outdated equipment may be starting to place the company at a competitive disadvantage. Ford found Jaguar's factory to be very underinvested and had to stomach high post-acquisition costs

- *Surplus assets.* There may be fixed-asset investments in non-core activities that could easily be disposed of without harming the mainstream business

- *Inadequate provisioning.* For example, the terms of business may provide generous warranties, but the balance sheet may suggest insufficient provision for likely warranty costs

- *Potential litigation.* Board minutes and minutes of more informal management meetings may reveal potential litigation for which no provision has been made in the accounts

Taxation

The FDD team is often asked to undertake a high level review of a target's tax affairs and highlight areas which appear likely to cause concern such as a dispute with the tax authorities. Any full tax investigation needs to be carried out by appropriate tax specialists. Make sure that the efforts of your various advisers are joined up, otherwise you risk increasing costs while not necessarily obtaining a better result.

The due diligence process should seek to identify tax planning opportunities both within the target and associated with the acquisition itself.

The following are examples of taxation issues that might be raised by FDD investigations:

- *Transfer pricing.* Transfer pricing where there is intra-group trading across different tax jurisdictions is a nightmare and needs a very thorough understanding to avoid nasty shocks later

- *Loan finance.* Loan finance provided to or by the target where it is made across different tax jurisdictions

- *Management fees.* Any management fees, in particular where the fees are made across tax jurisdictions

- *Tax credits.* Any tax credits arising on investments in research and development in case they are brought into question

- *Tax losses*. Tax losses which are presented as a future benefit to the acquirer can be a tricky negotiating point on a transaction. The vendor will of course try to sell these, but the acquirer, quite rightly, may not pay, arguing that there is no likely value to the vendor and their value to the acquirer is uncertain

- *Tax management possibilities*. Creative tax structures might be possible, for example there could be scope for implementing a structure in which interest on loan finance is tax deductible twice or even three times across international jurisdictions.

Financial issues relating to pension schemes

Understanding the target's pension arrangements and obtaining clear and up-to-date information on the future costs expected to be met by the company, are essential parts of FDD. The pension fund can be worth more than the target company. Equally, pension costs may be incurred many years into the future – and long after the workforce for whom the pensions are provided has ceased to be employed.

Issues that may need to be addressed include:

- *Valuation*. The valuation and funding of final salary pension schemes, including the basis of valuation according to actuarial schemes

- *Unfunded liabilities*. The existence of any unfunded pension promised to individual employees or directors

- *Contingent liabilities*. Contingent liabilities arising from changes in legislation not currently allowed for

- *Compliance with the rules*. Existing compliance with all aspects of pensions legislation and regulation

- *Post-acquisition pension arrangements*. Proposals for provision of past and future service pension benefits post-acquisition

- *Transitional arrangements*, and

- *Expectations*. Employment rights and expectations of target workforce

Much of the information required for the due diligence investigation will be available from the following sources:

- Trust deeds and rules for all schemes, including amendments

- Members' explanatory booklets and any announcements

- Annual trustees' reports and accounts for the scheme, latest and previous years

- Company accounts (pension scheme costs and disclosures), and

- Actuarial valuation reports, latest and previous one, plus any related correspondence on the actuarial position

Buyers and sellers often tangle over the net worth of the pension scheme as an asset or liability of the business. Specialist actuarial advice is therefore essential. The buyer may need to commission its own independent calculations, so it is important that the question of pensions is flagged up early in the process.

Financial projections

The logical finishing point for FDD is a review of the target company's financial projections. Often the review of financial projections falls into two parts:

- An estimate or projection for the current year based on the latest management accounting information, together with any information on sales in the near future

- A review of the projected performance for two to five years following the year in progress. This will rely on a heavy input from the CDD team

Get opinions, not just facts

When selecting an investigating accountant it is important to discuss the strength of opinion that he will be prepared to give on the financial projections. Accountants are worried about being sued; as a result they may just describe the projections, whilst the acquirer actually needs a view on their quality. At least they should give comfort on the level of care that has gone into preparing the projections and say if the major assumptions are based on sound judgements.

Preparation of the projections

Before reviewing the projections the investigating accountant should look at the background to their preparation, looking into issues such as:

- *The target's past experience of preparing forecast financial information.* For example is there a formal, corporate budgeting process? In some owner-managed businesses there may be no formal budget, or there may just be a sales objective, which is not used to run the business

- *Accuracy of past forecasts.* The target may have always failed to meet its forecasts suggesting that the current forecasts may not be achieved either

- *Involvement of those who will deliver the forecast.* The team that prepared the forecasts may not be closely involved in the operational management of the target. Has the forecast been prepared by a head office running the sale of the target, without the involvement of the local management?

- *The influence of any earn-outs.* Earn-outs can impact the motivation of those involved in the preparation of the forecasts. For instance, a vendor may even be inclined to understate likely future performance hoping to negotiate an unchallenging earn-out target.

Forecasts often predict a step change in the target's performance. This must be challenged and tested in order to identify where their weaknesses lie and realistic revisions made as necessary.

Link with commercial due diligence

CDD is strongly focused on market, competitive position and future performance. It is on the question of future sales that the investigating accountant feels most vulnerable and ill-equipped to comment, once again underlining the need for close cooperation between the CDD and the FDD teams.

The review of the forecasts

In addition to reviewing the CDD reports the investigating accountant will seek to gain comfort on the forecasts by:

- Careful analysis of past performance compared with the forecast
- Looking for as much solid supporting evidence of sales as possible, for example has the price increase already been agreed with customers? If not, what is the past success of introducing price increases, and what is the pricing policy of competitors?
- Looking into selling prices, purchase prices and product costs to establish margin pressures. Where does the power lie in the target's relationship with its suppliers – which is more dependent on the other, and so who is in the driving seat?
- Reviewing in detail the forecast overheads compared to historical overheads

Acquisition synergies

Forecasts are usually prepared on a stand-alone basis, without taking into account the impact of new ownership. In some cases the acquirer and the target may work together to incorporate synergies into the forecast with FDD incorporating a review of these forecast synergies and the costs of their implementation.

Figure 5.6 shows how the CDD and FDD combine to build a view of forecasts.

Legal investigations

What is legal due diligence?

Legal due diligence ensures that the future prospects of the target have a sound legal base. For example, 'change of control clauses' in key contracts, which are quite common in debt or lease contracts as well as in substantial supplier contracts, can be a two-edged sword. They may help the business to take big steps forward, but when invoked they risk negotiation of key contractual terms.

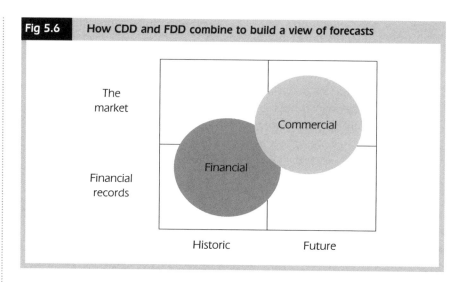

Fig 5.6   How CDD and FDD combine to build a view of forecasts

Of the three main due diligence disciplines, legal is the one most concerned with getting transactions done. Not surprisingly it is intimately bound up with the negotiation of the final sale and purchase agreement between buyer and seller. Appendix C contains a legal due diligence check list which sets out the issues it should cover. As can be seen, it is mostly concerned with verifying assets and liabilities and making sure the target can legally complete the transaction. This might sound odd but the sale of a company can require certain consents or releases such as a release of the target company's shares from a parent company debenture, clearances from merger control authorities, approvals from significant suppliers or customers and releases or rollover of employees' share options.

Some of these hidden requirements for consents may not be immediately obvious, but failing to follow the correct procedure can be messy and expensive to sort out later. This does not mean that legal due diligence is a tick-box exercise. Like all forms of due diligence it is carried out primarily with an eye on the future. It does this, for example, by ensuring that:

- The target has appropriate rights over intellectual property
- Appropriate supplier and customer contracts are in place and are secure
- Appropriate employment contracts are in place
- The target complies with all legislation relevant to its current and planned activities
- There are no major disputes in progress which could lead to costly, time-consuming battles post-acquisition

Why do it?

When the buyer and seller sign the legal agreement which sets out the terms on which the acquisition is completed, it will contain various legally-enforceable guarantees that the company's affairs are what the seller says they are. These warranties and indemnities, as they are known, theoretically mean that an acquirer could avoid legal investigations altogether. The reason most buyers do not follow this route is that if things go wrong, the seller has the money, and the buyer may well have to litigate. Litigation is costly, time-consuming, distracting and success is far from certain and even if it is successful, the acquirer is almost sure to be out of pocket. As a rule of thumb, the acquirer is only likely to recover 50–65 per cent of its costs. It is far better to identify problems and 'deal breakers' early and include them in the valuation and price negotiations.

From the buyer's perspective, the nature and quality of the seller's representations and warranties, like all negotiated provisions of the agreement, are dependent on the respective bargaining power of the parties. The seller will be reluctant to make blanket representations that may allow the buyer to terminate the agreement prior to closing or lead to it paying damages.

Accordingly, the seller should encourage the buyer to use due diligence to replace its perceived need for blanket protection. The buyer will in any case also be keen to carry out an extensive due diligence as a substitute for extensive representations and warranties. As due diligence relies extensively on information provided by the seller, the buyer will look for assurances in the agreement that the information it has been provided is both comprehensive and correct.

Apart from checking out hard facts, legal due diligence can unearth previously unidentified problems. These arise when a seller genuinely believes the target company is problem-free and clean but a due diligence programme uncovers difficulties. Typically the seller is not being dishonest or attempting to mislead, but simply does not have the necessary professional skills to spot a legal problem. The acquisition of a software company is a good example of where this might arise. It is normal for chunks of code to be written by outside contractors. The law is clear on who owns the copyright to such code. Unless assigned, it belongs to the author. As far as the seller is concerned a product exists which works and which is generating revenue. As far as the buyer is concerned, he or she is being asked to pay good money for a firm which does not own the rights to all of its product.

Where does LDD get the information?

There are a number of steps in a typical legal due diligence process. These are:

- Site visits
- Written questionnaires
- Data room visits
- Disclosure letter
- Certificates of title
- Commissioning specialist reports
- Collection of public information

Site visits

The legal team will inevitably want to visit the premises of the target company personally. The reason for this is that top management can prove more willing than the shareholders to disclose some matters to the acquirer. You should resist sellers' attempts to restrict access, although the lawyer must be sensitive to confidentiality and the circumstances of the transaction.

Written questionnaires

Next the legal team will send a list of highly-detailed written questions to the seller covering the issues on the checklist in Appendix C. As mentioned in the previous section, standard information requests should be adapted to the specifics of the transaction and all information requests from advisers should be coordinated in order to avoid duplication and confusion.

Data room visits

If there are a number of potential acquirers, the seller may put together a data room where information about the target business is collected for all potential acquirers to review. The objective is to give potential acquirers sufficient information to enable them to submit indicative bids for the target company. The preferred bidder will usually be allowed to conduct a normal due diligence programme once selected. The depth and quality of information available in data rooms is highly varied. Do not expect too much, otherwise you will be disappointed.

Disclosure letter

At some stage the seller will 'disclose' against the legal questions. It is in the seller's interest to disclose as much as possible because what the buyer finds out this way cannot be the subject of legal action later on. Disclosure letters are therefore themselves a source of due diligence information. For example, they will contain a list of current and pending litigation.

While we are on the subject, the disclosure letter invariably goes through a succession of drafts, each one disclosing more information – and possibly leading to more questions about the information disclosed, seeking further and better particulars. Make sure that the seller does not deliver the disclosure letter at the eleventh hour. At this point the word 'letter' may be misleading anyway, because on large or very complex transactions, it may be closer to the size of a filing cabinet! If the final disclosure letter contains new information this can derail the completion, as the buyer may need to reconsider some aspects of the deal. Early drafting of the final disclosure letter helps to keep the due diligence process within the timetable.

Certificates of title

Acquirers need to know if the target company has the title to its properties. A shortcut can be to arrange for the target's solicitors to deliver certificates of title. This can be quicker and cheaper than an investigation because the solicitors concerned already know the information. Another advantage is the professional indemnity insurance cover of the solicitors giving the certificate.

Commissioning specialist reports

Specialist advisers may be needed to report on particular aspects of the business, such as environmental risk assessment. These reports have a long lead time, so they should be commissioned early. Access to the premises may also need to be agreed.

Collection of public information

The investigation should also cover information from public sources. The acquirer is not reliant on the cooperation of the seller for this information and can verify the information which the seller provides itself. The most important public information sources are set out in Appendix D.

How much LDD is needed?

Legal due diligence reports do not have to cover every aspect of the target's affairs. As with other forms of due diligence, the trick is to concentrate on the most important areas. These will be:

- Understanding what you do not already know about the major potential risks
- Verifying the underlying ability of the business to deliver the profits assumed in the valuation model

An acquirer in the same market as the target may feel more relaxed about the level and scope of due diligence required than, say, a private equity investor. Professional advisers are famous for expanding their scope of work so they can increase fees and lawyers above all appreciate that you cannot get sued for doing too much.

Conclusion

Due diligence is not just about checking that the target is what you thought it was. Commercial, financial and legal due diligence, and their sub-specialisms, should all concentrate on the future of the business as well as on the immediate risks and mechanics of doing the deal.

Due diligence should have five strands to it to prevent it being an expensive waste of time and money. These are:

- The verification of assets and liabilities
- The identification and quantification of risks
- The protection needed against these risks in the form of price adjustments and warranties and indemnities

and most important of all:

- The identification/confirmation of synergy benefits
- Post-acquisition planning

Due diligence is not a clever legal or financial exercise. It involves a lot of people digging up a lot of often incomplete and conflicting information in a very short time. The challenge for the person who commissions due diligence is to stay on top of all this by not getting lost in the detail, having the insight and experience to spot what is important and what is not and, above all, project-managing the exercise. As with most things, best value is obtained by having the right people doing the right things at the right time in the right way. Only meticulous planning and excellent management will do. Doing deals is sexy, doing due diligence is not, which is why it is so often badly planned and badly managed with predictably disappointing results.

Valuation 6

Valuation is no mystery. The trap that people can fall into is thinking that there is a single mathematical route to calculating value and one single, 'right', number applicable to a company's value. There is no single number and no right number. It is an old cliché but the value of a company is the price agreed between a willing buyer and a willing seller. Value, then, can only be worked out in hindsight, which is not much good if you are the person struggling to calculate a price for an indicative offer prior to a deal.

Let us first of all deal with a couple of the myths of valuation and then turn to how to do it in practice.

Valuation is not best left to the experts

Valuation is not difficult if you understand the techniques and principles. It should certainly not be just handed over to the consultants or experts. The benefit of being fully involved with the valuation process is that it forces you to get down to the details of what drives the value of the target company, where those drivers are going, where the synergies are going to come from and how they are going to be realised. The M&A market is very efficient. Good deals are hard to come by and will result only from highly disciplined deal making, including really understanding what it is you are buying and just how you are going to add value to the business and so recoup the premium you will pay. It also tells you where the risks are.

There is no single number

There is no such thing as the correct valuate of a business. 'Value' is the amount a purchaser is willing to pay for the business. This can vary enormously: the evidence shows that when at least four provisional written offers are made for a business, the highest one is likely to be at least 50 per cent more than the lowest offer. Occasionally it can be more than double. Clearly buyers and sellers are going to have very different ideas about value. You will come up with a different number depending on whether you are buying or selling. But, you might ask, how can this be when both sides are working from the same data and using the same valuation methods? The answer is they are doing neither. Each one will use valuation methods that give the best answer. For example a seller is going to be very interested in multiples achieved by previous sellers because these establish the nearest thing there is to 'market value'. The buyer on the other hand, at least if rational, will want to pay the lowest possible price but one which is high enough to persuade the owners to sell and which is more than anyone else is willing to pay. In turn this means offering a price which is enough to persuade the sellers and anyone else who might be interested that it is willing to pay more than they think the business is worth. The buyer's upper limit is what the business is worth to it. There is absolutely no point in a buyer paying more.

A good example of acquisition pricing in action is the bid for William Low by Tesco in 1994 when shareholders benefited by £93 m – an uplift of 60 per cent on the original Tesco offer – thanks to Sainsbury's.

After hard negotiating Tesco made an initial offer of 225p per share. This valued the company at £154 m, it was accepted by William Low and that would have been the end of the story, had J Sainsbury not intervened. J Sainsbury launched a hostile bid at 305p per share topping Tesco's offer by 35.5 per cent and valuing William Low at £210 m. It was widely believed that Sainsbury's only motive for entering the bidding was to drive up the price for Tesco. However Tesco's advisers recognised that Sainsbury would not have entered without willingness to take the business on.

Tesco's management was convinced that their greater presence and experience in the region put them in the best position to obtain maximum value out of William Low. They decided to make a second offer of 360p, topping the first by no less than 60 per cent, valuing the Scottish supermarket operator at £247 m.

Therefore, do not be seduced by complex mathematical modelling. Instead bear in mind that:

- A buyer in exclusive negotiations has every chance of obtaining a better deal
- The shareholders of a seller are better off if there are competing buyers
- The value of a company is whatever a buyer is prepared to pay for it. In this case, William Low was worth £93 m more to Tesco than its original offer had indicated
- There is no rule as to what price a company is worth or will be sold for

The valuation process – a summary

The valuation process described above is summarised (and considerably simplified) in Figure 6.1. This shows the process as having three steps:

- Establish an intrinsic value i.e. the value of the business as a standalone entity. To do this the buyer needs to project its underlying performance and thereby estimate future profits and cash flows. At the same time the buyer should also assess the realisable value of any surplus assets as these will add to the valuation

- Assess synergy benefits – in detail. These are the source of value you the buyer will add to the business and the justification for the premium you are inevitably going to pay. If you cannot say where these benefits are going to come from or how they are going to be realised you should be asking yourself not just how much you should pay for the company but whether you should be acquiring it at all

- Factor in transaction costs and reorganisation costs. Both of these can be considerable but are often underestimated or even forgotten in the heat of the transaction[1]

Assuming there is such a thing as an 'intrinsic' value for the business, a subject to which we will return later, the buyer will be willing to pay up to a maximum of this intrinsic value plus any post-acquisition synergies available to it. This must be more than other potential purchasers are willing to pay, otherwise it will be outbid. It must also be more than the seller thinks that the business is worth, or it will seek alternative buyers or not sell. For example, Pearson abandoned the sale of its business publishing arm in 2002 after a very public auction and MBO attempt because it reckoned that all the various offers were less than the value it could extract from the business.

What the seller thinks the business is worth is somewhere between the intrinsic value of the business and what he thinks the market will pay. Fashion can improve the market value of a business considerably while desperation to sell quickly or a previous sale that did not go through can create soiled goods whose market value is depressed.

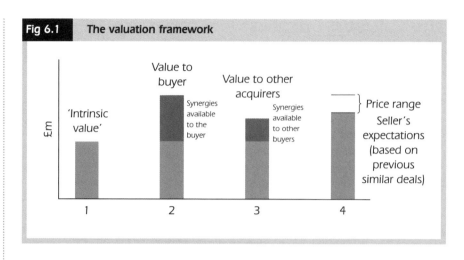

Fig 6.1 The valuation framework

Valuation is not just about modelling

Another reason we can never say that a business is worth £x or €y is that valuations have a habit of changing. Often this is to do with expectations about the underlying performance of the business. A business, after all, is bought for its future performance and, as stock market movements show, expectations of the future change on a daily basis. Sellers of Internet or telecoms businesses in 1998/99 got some very good prices indeed. By March 2000 they would be lucky to find any buyers at all. Referring back to Figure 6.1, the size of column 1, which after all is nothing more than the expectation of future performance translated into current value, fell considerably as did the size of column 4. Why? Who knows, except that by March 2000 potential buyers had probably got enough of a feel for Internet companies to realise that they could not live up to the expectations built into their valuations.

It should be clear from this example that expectations are everything. But expectations are not hard facts. Sure they can be dressed up as hard facts by being represented as numbers but when all is said and done, they are someone's assessment of what they think is going to happen. So, before the potential buyer or seller opens its spreadsheet it has to have a view on the future. There are a number of ways in which some of the uncertainty in the future can be reduced, such as using a real options approach to valuation,[2] but all acquirers should recognise that valuation has too many subjective elements to it to make it a coldly rational mathematical process.

Businesses are bought for their future prospects. History alone will not tell you about the future, but history cannot not be ignored all together. First it will give you a starting point for projections. History will also put the forecasts into context. If gross margin has been shrinking for five years is there not something extraordinary happening in a forecast if the trend suddenly starts to reverse? Erratic profits and losses during the last three years will tell you that a smoothly progressing 'hockey stick' projection is nonsense. Historic overhead costs will tell you what scope there is for cost savings if two businesses are to be brought together.

To really understand the future you have to understand the fundamentals. This means getting down to the details of:

- What is happening in the market?
- Can this company continue to compete effectively?
- How big are those synergy benefits?, and
- How are we going to realise them post-acquisition?

The other reason why valuation is more than just numbers is to do with the gap between columns 2 and 4 in Figure 6.1. The size of that gap is purely a matter of negotiation. Ideally the buyer does not want to give away any of the synergy benefits available. Why should it when it is the only one that can actually realise them? On the other hand, the seller knows that the company is worth more to the buyer than it thinks it is worth and will therefore be keen to get a share of the synergies.

Sadly for buyers the evidence suggests that they are either not very good at negotiating the premium above 'intrinsic value' or (and we suspect this is really the case) cannot add much in the way of value to the acquisitions they do make. Work done in this area suggests that sellers do much better than buyers in an acquisition.

Calculating synergies

Synergies are easier to imagine than to realise. Acquirers and advisers routinely exaggerate the amount of synergy to be had and the speed with which it can be captured. It is essential to calculate in as much detail as possible the size of each hoped for synergy benefit and precisely how and over what period each will be unlocked and by whom. It is not good enough to accept the bland assertion of ambitious directors or incentivised advisers for example that '10 per cent of combined overheads can be saved'. It is also important to remember that many synergies come at a cost – a new computer system or redundancy costs. The one-off costs of achieving synergy benefits have to be calculated too. Once calculated, benefits arising from synergy should be shown separately otherwise there is a risk that these benefits will be negotiated away.

Valuation techniques

With so much emphasis placed on negotiating, judgement and horse-trading, why are numeric-based valuation techniques so important? The answer is that you have to start somewhere. Acquirers need to use valuation models to calculate a realistic expectation of the worth of a business and sellers do not usually indicate an asking price until they have received a detailed written offer.

The traditional techniques to consider are (in approximate order of utility):

1 Discounted cash flow (DCF)

2 Return on investment

3 Price/Earnings (P/E) and other profit ratios

4 Comparable transactions

5 Sector-specific valuation benchmarks

6 Impact on earnings per share

7 Net asset backing

Having examined these techniques in detail, we will then go on to consider some of the techniques used to value special cases. An example of a special case might be a start-up company that does not have a trading record or has a particularly strong portfolio of brands.

Choosing the valuation method

Empirical research suggests that cash flow, not accounting earnings, drives value.[3] In the earnings approach, companies are valued based on a multiple of accounting earnings. Or in other words a multiple of the profit figure calculated by the accountants, as opposed to the hard cash it made. In effect this earnings method is saying a number of things which do not make sense:

- Only last year's, this year's or next year's earnings matter. A single P/E ratio cannot possibly capture an entire business cycle

- The timing of returns does not matter. A company which has done badly this year, and will recover next year, could be valued the same as one which has done exceptionally well

- The investment required to generate those earnings does not matter. In other words, if two companies produce the same earnings they should be valued the same, regardless of the resources required to generate earnings. This has to be nonsense. Does the Building Society offer you the same cash interest on deposits of £50 as it does on deposits of £100?

- Different accounting treatments do not matter. They do. The classic example was of Daimler's accounts at the time of the Chrysler merger. Under German GAAP profits were DM1 bn. Under US GAAP this was transformed into a US$1 bn loss
- Different financial structures do not matter. They do. Gearing increases potential reward to shareholders but also increases risk. In the DCF approach, the value of the business is the expected cash flow discounted at a rate that reflects the riskiness of the cash flow
- Short-term stock market prices reflect a company's intrinsic value. They do not. There is an awful lot of speculation wrapped up in a share price

Use more than one method

Because there is no such thing as a true value, both buyers and sellers will use more than one technique. Three techniques is often held to be a good number as this allows a triangulation on value, see Figure 6.2 below.

Another reason for using more than one method is to give a reference point. Reference points might be given by prices paid in similar deals such as the multiple of operating profit (acquisition price divided by operating profit) or the multiple of EBITDA (earnings before interest, tax, depreciation and amortisation). EBITDA is often used as a surrogate for cash flow. These can at least reassure the buyer that the agreed price is in line with 'market' price.

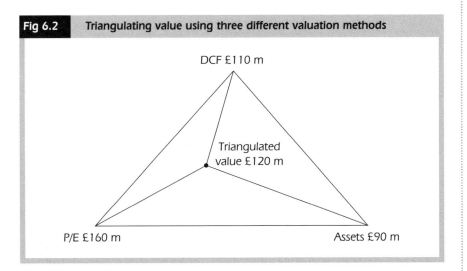

Fig 6.2 Triangulating value using three different valuation methods

DCF £110 m

Triangulated value £120 m

P/E £160 m   Assets £90 m

1: Discounted cash flow (DCF)

The DCF approach says that value is added if an investment generates a return which is more than can be generated elsewhere for the same risk. That sounds like it might be complicated but all it is really saying is that if the going rate for ultra safe instant access deposits is 4 per cent and you can get 5 per cent, go for it. Similarly, if the going rate for return on investments in electric-arc slab cast steelmaking in Eastern Europe is 10 per cent and you think you can get 11 per cent, then you should go ahead with the investment.

The process

Assumptions

Some maintain the cash flow approach suffers less from the subjectivity that bedevils other valuation methods as it makes explicit assumptions and estimates. Others regard it as just as subjective and error-prone. According to one leading UK Private Equity investor DCF actually stands for 'Deceit by Computer Forecast'.

As ever, the truth lies somewhere between the two. DCF does rely on a whole host of assumptions and valuations can be moved by significant amounts depending on the assumptions or how the maths is done. On the other hand, DCF does force the acquirer to look in detail at the particulars of the investment and this is its main advantage. Unlike the other approaches, it encourages the explicit estimation of:

- Sales volumes and prices. These are rarely as smooth and positive as presented in an information memorandum
- The cost base. An acquisition may give better purchasing power or spread fixed costs over a bigger sales volume
- Individual profit streams. Companies rarely sell one homogenous product to the same group of buyers. DCF forces the buyer to consider all the different profit streams. Often these have very different characteristics
- Any additional capital expenditure that may be required. Businesses are often sold because they have reached a point where they need new investment or a new approach. Alternatively, they are often bought to achieve economies of scale by rationalising operations so that lower levels of capital expenditure may be needed once the initial rationalisation has been carried out
- Changes in working capital, reflecting, for example, turnover growth or better financial management

Because you have to project sales and profits forward for five or ten years, DCF forces you to understand the underlying economic value drivers of the business to arrive at a value. The resulting computer model then gives the platform for carrying out sensitivity analyses to assess the impact of changes in assumptions.

Computer modelling

PCs allow very detailed computer models. There is always a danger that analysts get so deep into the details that they miss the bigger picture.

The general rules for building computer models need to be kept in mind. Models should be sufficiently well planned and documented for someone else to be able to understand and use. Other generally-accepted conventions are:

- Assumptions and other numbers which might be flexed, for example the cost of financing, should be explicitly stated in a section of their own

- There should be only one source for each number. This means that numbers which are input are done so only once and if used in more than one location in the spreadsheet, for example in different versions of the model, they are read across into the other sections. If numbers are calculated in one section and used in another these should also be read across. This not only minimises the likelihood of keying errors but also provides an audit trail

- The base year should be reconciled back to statutory or management accounts. It is best to have a run of three to five years' history with key ratios calculated for each year to act as a sanity check on the model's projection of these same ratios

- DCF models should be designed to calculate balance sheet values. If the balance sheet does not balance you know there is something wrong. To do this the model must calculate cash flows for every period and adjust the closing debt figure in the last period by the amount of the cash generated. If cash is independently calculated this way and not, as some accountants favour, simply taken as the difference between two balance sheets, you have a check that the model is working correctly

One financial analyst modelled a large public company which was not performing well. He proudly took the results to the chairman and informed him that he had nothing to worry about as the company could easily afford all the capital expenditure needed over the coming years. The chairman looked up from the figures and told him that, while he was very impressed with all his computer handy work, sadly capital expenditure meant paying out money, not receiving it. A simple mistake in the model meant that the sign for capital expenditure was the wrong way round.

A mathematical check does not, of course, dispense with the need for sanity checks:

- Capital expenditure is an expense, as is an increase in stock and an increase in debtors
- There tend to be industry norms for most ratios
- Margins tend to erode over time
- Selling prices tend to fall over time

The maths

The mathematics behind discounting is much simpler than all those squiggles in the formulae would suggest. A few minutes invested in understanding the basic principles, however unappealing that may sound, is well worth the (limited) brain power needed. All you need to know about discounting is set out in the following 300 or so simple words.

Lend me a pound and I'll pay you back with interest this time next year. At the present interest rate of about 4 per cent you would expect to get £1.04 back.

Now turn that proposition round. I'll give you a pound this time next year if you give me 95p now. Is this a good deal? Yes it is for you, because if you put that 95p in the bank it would be worth only 98.8p twelve months hence. You would be much better off lending it to me and getting £1 back, assuming you regard lending to me as no more risky than lending to a bank. Suppose I offered you £1 in twelve months for 97p now? This is not a good deal. At 4 per cent interest, 97p would be worth £1.0088 in a year and as an astute financier you would negotiate the 97p down to 96.1538p.

Interest rates are going to stick at 4 per cent. How much would you give me now if I promise to give you £1 in two years' time? The answer is roughly 92½p. Your logic would be

Value now	Value next year	Value the year after
92.4556	96.1538	£1

Because

92.4556p invested for one year at 4 per cent is worth 96.1538p
(= 92.4556 × 1.04)˙

and

96.1538p invested for a further year at 4 per cent is worth £1 (= 96.1538 × 1.04)

but because you need to calculate the value today of the £1 you will receive two years hence, you need to invert the calculation.

Value now	Value next year	Value the year after
(£1 ÷ 1.04) ÷ 1.04 = 92.4556	£1 ÷ 1.04 = 96.1538	£1

This is the principal behind discounting, but it is always made to look much more complicated as we can see from the normal discounting formula:

$$PV = \sum \frac{CF_t}{(1 + r)^t}$$

All the formula is saying is that the present value of a business (PV) is the sum of each year's free cash flow (CF_t) divided by 1 plus the discount rate (1 + r) raised to the power of the year number in question (t), which when expanded looks like this:

$$PV = \frac{CF_1}{1 + r} + \frac{CF_2}{(1 + r)^2} + \frac{CF_3}{(1 + r)^3}$$

Which with cash flows of £100, £200 and £250 and a discount rate of 7 per cent (based on an assumption of base rate plus 3 per cent risk) looks like this:

$$PV = \frac{100}{1.07} + \frac{200}{1.07^2} + \frac{250}{1.07^3}$$

$$PV = 472.22$$

Free cash flow

Free cash flow does not mean 'not paid for' but cash which the company is free to use as it pleases; it is:

> Profit before interest and tax with non-cash charges (such as depreciation) added back
>
> *Less*
>
> Investments in operating assets such as working capital, property, plant and equipment

It does not include any financing related cash flows such as interest or dividends paid or received. Many people find this a hard concept to grasp, but it is easily understood if it is related to everyday experience. Imagine you are buying a house. Would you expect to pay more if you were funding part of the purchase with a mortgage? Would you expect to pay less? No, you would expect to pay the same whether you used all cash, all debt or a mixture of the two. Why, then, would you keep debt in a DCF calculation? What a business is worth and how you fund it are two completely separate decisions. A house is worth what a willing buyer and a willing seller decide it is worth. That value is not different if the buyer pays cash or takes out a 100 per cent mortgage. The same with companies. DCF values the company based on future cash flows generated by the business from operations. Just like in house buying, whether the business takes out loans or uses equity to finance itself is totally irrelevant to the basic valuation of the business as a going concern. Table 6.1 below shows how free cash is calculated.

Table 6.1	Calculating free cash flow for the valuation model	
	Operating profit	100
Plus	Depreciation	29
Less	Profit on the sale of fixed assets	(1)
Plus/(Less)	Decrease/(increase in stock)	(35)
Plus/(Less)	Decrease/(increase in debtors)	(20)
Plus/(Less)	Increase/(decrease in creditors)	9
=	**Net Cash Flow from continuing operations**	**82**
Less	Investment in fixed assets	(21)
Less	Investment in subsidiaries	–
Plus	Cash from sale of fixed assets	2
Plus	Cash from sale of investments	–
=	**Cash flow before financing and tax**	**63**

Using the right numbers

Before we can start to project free cash flows we must remove as many account-ing adjustments as possible from the numbers. The cleaned-up numbers will form the basis of our projections. In an ideal world, profits will equal cash. In most sets of accounts the two numbers are very different. There are good rea-sons for this, the need to build stock because of growth for example, and there are other reasons. The application of accounting policies can have a huge impact on reported numbers. Getting the 'right' set of numbers for a DCF model is often a case of undoing what accountants have done to the figures. The accounting policies of the acquirer – for example, the treatment of items such as depreciation and the valuation of work in progress – may be different from what the acquirer regards as appropriate.

The next set of adjustments that may be needed is taking out (or adding in) what may be termed exceptional costs. Chief amongst these in private compa-nies are realistic rewards for the directors – for example, lower salaries to bring them into line with other directors in group subsidiaries; the savings resulting from the termination of contracts of those relatives employed in the business and no longer required; eliminating the cost of unnecessary extravagances such as aeroplanes, boats and overseas homes enjoyed by directors.

Finally, as DCF is concerned with operating cash flow and therefore operat-ing assets, all non-operating assets need to be removed.

The particularly troublesome adjustments are listed below. Please note that some of these will not have a direct effect on the discounted cash flow calcula-tion, but they are needed either to 'clean up' the base of the DCF model or play a part in the final valuation calculation.

Fixed assets. As already mentioned, fixed assets should include only assets used in the operations of the business. Excluded from any projections would be investments in, say, marketable securities.

Operating leases. Operating leases represent a type of financing and, if mate-rial, should be treated as such. To do this they should be capitalised as follows:

- Deduct interest from the interest charge in the P&L
- Add the implied principal amount both to fixed assets and to debt. Dividing the interest charge by the interest rate is usually a good proxy for the prin-cipal amount

Pension deficits and surpluses. Treat a surplus or deficit on the pension scheme as:

- For a surplus – a loan given
- For a deficit – a loan taken out

Charge interest through the profit and loss as normal. In order for the balance sheet to continue to balance the retained earnings should be recalculated.

Provisions. Provisions charged through the profit and loss account are either reserves set up to fund future costs or losses or provisions to smooth future earnings. Either way they should be reversed out of the P&L and actual cash costs charged when/if they are incurred.

Capitalised expenses. In many ways these are similar to provisions and should be treated in the same way. All costs should be charged as they are incurred. The argument that these have a future benefit does not wash here. If they do have a future benefit, this will be reflected in sales and profits.

Working capital. This is operating working capital, usually stock, trade creditors, trade debtors and some cash. A 'reasonable' cash balance is put at 0.5 to 2.0 per cent of sales.[4] Excess cash balances would have to be excluded (and included on the financing side of the balance sheet).

Tax. Adjust to a cash basis, which can normally be done by adjusting the annual tax charge on the P&L by changes in the deferred tax position (to adjust for capital allowances and such like) and in changes in the tax debtors figure (as most taxes are paid after the year end).

Tax losses. Tax losses can be extremely important to the viability of a transaction and justifying it internally. The reality is that they can easily be lost. Try to make them contingent and do not be tempted to include the value of tax losses in the valuation (or anything other than contingent in the price you negotiate).

Nominal or real numbers?[5] Nominal! You try working in real numbers (easy for sales and costs but not for assets) and then explaining to the Chairman why he does not recognise any of the figures.

Pre-tax or post-tax? Normally, discounted cash flow valuations use post-tax cash flows. That is what corresponds to 'free cash flow' i.e. cash which the company is free to do what it wants with. In truth it does not matter whether the cash flows are taxed or untaxed, as long as the discount rate used is consistent. If you use taxed cash flow, then the discount rate needs to be reduced by the tax effect which means that the cost of debt in the cost of capital should be multiplied by 1 minus the tax rate.

The discount rate

DCF uses the acquirer's cost of capital as the discount rate. Easily said but small percentage movements in the discount rate can move the valuation by many millions and there is no real scientific answer to what is the right rate.[6] Logical application of a thorough understanding of the principles is therefore the key. First of all:

- The cost of capital is the weighted average cost of capital (WACC) of all sources of capital. Each cost should reflect the risk each is taking (more on that below)
- The weighting should be at market rates – but should reflect target rather than actual proportions
- Costs should be after tax if cash flows are computed after tax
- Rates are expressed in nominal terms, because cash flows are stated in nominal terms

The formula is the cost of equity plus the after-tax cost of debt, as follows:

$$WACC(r) = K_D\,(1 - T)\,\frac{D}{D + E} + K_E\,\frac{E}{D + E}$$

Where:
K_E = Cost of equity
K_D = Cost of debt
T = Acquirer's effective tax rate
D = Market value of debt
E = Market value of equity

The cost of debt

The cost of debt should be fairly straightforward to calculate, although hybrid forms may complicate matters. The cost of debt is annual interest payment divided by the market value of the debt. Always use market values where possible. If the instrument is not-traded the following applies:

- Identify the payments to be made
- Estimate the credit quality (somewhere between AAA and junk)
- Look up the yield to maturity on similarly rated traded bonds with similar coupons and maturities
- Calculate the approximate market value by finding the present value of the future payments using the yield to maturity on the traded instrument as the discount rate

The cost of preferred stock should lie between debt and equity.

The cost of equity

Determining the cost of equity is always an issue. Equity should be valued using market prices where possible. If the acquirer is not quoted it will have to use figures from comparable companies which are quoted. The cost of equity to a company is the return that an investor expects from it. To cut a long story very short, there are two shortcuts that help arrive at a number:

- The return on an equity comprises a risk free rate plus a premium for risk, and

- The returns on an individual stock are related to the return on the market as a whole

The yield on a ten-year government bond is the best estimate of the risk free rate and the historical equity risk premium is in the 4.5 to 5 per cent range. This gives an average return on the market as a whole. Getting from this to the cost of equity for a particular stock calls for the use of betas.

Betas derive from the theory that returns on all individual shares are related to returns on the market as a whole. Again to cut a long story very short, the variability of returns on individual stocks are plotted relative to returns on the market and the beta is given by the point at which the stock in question lies on the slope of the line of best fit. This is illustrated in Figure 6.3. The beta for the market as a whole is 1. The more risky a stock is, the higher its beta will be. Fortunately we do not have to calculate betas ourselves because they are published on a regular basis by a number of financial data providers.

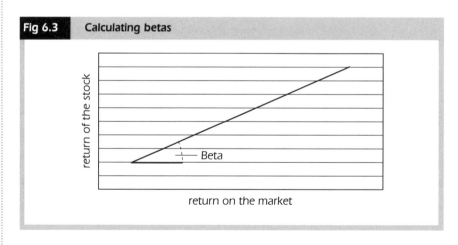

Fig 6.3   **Calculating betas**

The resulting beta is then fed into the following formula, which is not quite as fearsome as it looks, to arrive at the cost of equity:

$$K_E = R_F + \beta(R_N - R_F)$$

Where:
K_E = Cost of Equity
R_F = Risk Free Rate
β = Beta of the Acquirer
R_N = Return on the Market Portfolio

The value of convertible securities are a bit trickier since their value is made up partly of the interest received and partly by the conversion feature. Because the conversion feature has a value, the coupon rate is generally lower than with straight debt and therefore the cost lies somewhere between the cost of debt and the cost of equity.

A minority interest is a claim by outside shareholders on a portion of a company's business. It arises where the target company has sold a proportion of a subsidiary or made an acquisition and not bought out all of the shareholders. The value of a minority interest is related to the value of the underlying asset in which the minority partner has a stake. If there is no market value and cash flows are not available use a market value proxy, such as comparable company P/Es, to calculate market value.

Terminal value

An additional complication in DCF is that businesses go on forever, whereas cash flow forecasts are normally cut off after five or ten years. This is usually dealt with by dividing the forecast period into two:

- The explicit forecast period – the period you are trying to forecast in detail
- The period after the end of the explicit period to infinity, i.e. the period you are not trying to forecast in detail. This is often referred to as the 'terminal value' or the 'continuing value'

It is sometimes frightening how big the terminal value can be compared with the discounted cash flows for the forecast period. It stands to reason, therefore, that a careful estimate of terminal value is central to valuation. Normally a DCF model uses simplifying assumptions to calculate terminal value. The most popular are as follows:

- Discount terminal asset value – i.e. take the asset value in the final year and discount it back to today's value. Essentially this assumes liquidation at the end of the forecast period which may not be a sensible assumption to make

- The final year's cash flow is assumed to continue to perpetuity. The formula for calculating a value to perpetuity is:

$$\text{Final Year Free Cash Flow / WACC or } \frac{CF_t}{r}$$

The resulting value is then discounted back to the start of the model by multiplying by $\frac{1}{(1+r)^t}$. This assumes that the final year cash flow is sustainable to infinity.

- A variation on the above is used for growth stocks. Final year cash flow is calculated to infinity but there is an allowance for growth at a constant rate. The formula is:

$$\text{Final Year Free Cash Flow/(WACC – annual growth percentage (g)) or } \frac{CF_t}{r-g}$$

In other words the WACC is reduced by the assumed growth rate g leading to a lower denominator and a higher terminal value. Again the resulting value is discounted back to year zero.

DCF has a lot of advantages as a valuation tool and it does force prospective buyers into a rigorous examination of the business and its future performance. The downside is that, as already mentioned, the results from a DCF modelling exercise can move significantly with just a small change in some of the assumptions. Buyers, therefore, should use more than one approach to valuation, if only as a sanity check on the DCF. The other methods which could be used are set out below.

2: Return on investment

Return on investment provides a good safe target on which a valuation can be based. The downsides of the ROI approach are that it does not accommodate the cash implications of the deal and that it can be too broad-brush. On the other hand, acquisitions should not be treated any differently to other forms of capital expenditure so although companies are acquired for long-term strategic reasons, there should be an acceptable return on investment during the early years after acquisition.

The ROI approach to evaluating an acquisition is no different from the standard technique which would be used to appraise any other form of investment. Many large companies use the pre-tax return on capital employed to judge capital expenditure proposals and as a key measure of performance for each of their subsidiary companies. It is not surprising, therefore, that a similar approach is often used as a short-cut method to assess a prospective acquisition.

For comparative purposes with other capital projects this ratio is best kept free from the burden of costs of capital. Thus the profits to be used are prior to any of the funding costs of the acquisition.

ROI is calculated by taking forecast profit before tax in the second full financial year following acquisition, adjusting it for the effects of your ownership and dividing it by the total investment to date:

$$ROI = \frac{\textit{Adjusted pre-tax profit (for the second full year of ownership)}}{\textit{Total acquisition price + net cash invested in year 1}}$$

The second year is used to allow time for the acquisition to bed down – although it may be more relevant to use the third full year of profits if an earn-out deal has been structured to cover three years. The denominator should take into account the initial purchase consideration, any expected earn-out payments and the cash generated from the business or the amount of cash to be invested to achieve the forecast profit growth.

The answer gives a percentage pre-tax return on the proposed purchase price. It is difficult to set a reasonable benchmark.

Example

To determine maximum acquisition price.

- Acquisition made in 2005
- Acquirer expects adjusted profit before tax in 2007 of £2 m
- Additional cash investment required of £1 m by 2007

What is the maximum acquisition price (AP) to give 20 per cent return?

$$0.2 = \frac{2}{Total\ acquisition\ price(AP) + 1}$$

$$0.2(AP + 1) = 2$$

$$AP = \frac{2 - 0.2}{0.2}$$

Therefore maximum acquisition price = £9 m

3: Price/earnings and other profit ratios

Price/earnings ratios attempt to assess 'market value' and they provide a useful benchmark for sellers. Other profit ratios are a variation on this theme.

A listed company has a price/earnings ratio noted every day in the Financial Times, Wall Street Journal or elsewhere. The price earnings multiple of a listed company is the number of years of profit after tax per share is represented by the current share price. It comprises the following:

$$P/E = \frac{Current\ share\ price}{Earnings\ (profit\ after\ tax)\ per\ share}$$

or

$$P/E = \frac{Market\ capitalisation\ divided\ by\ number\ of\ shares}{Earnings\ divided\ by\ number\ of\ shares}$$

or

$$P/E = \frac{Market\ capitalisation}{Earnings}$$

P/E ratios are widely used, and with good reason. They are relatively quick and simple to apply and are readily verifiable. The P/E ratio applied to an unquoted target is derived from the P/E ratios of comparable quoted companies. By using quoted market prices they also build in current market expectations of performance. First find comparable quoted companies, then determine their P/Es and then apply these to an estimate of the sustainable earnings of the target. It sounds simple enough, but there are a number of complications that have to be adjusted for.

Public vs private P/E ratios

Using listed P/Es assumes that the target company could be floated. If the target company is not large enough for this or the conditions are not right, the likely price/earnings ratio should be reduced by between 30 to 40 per cent. The amount of the reduction should reflect the attractiveness of the particular business sector and the attractiveness of the target. The accountants BDO publish a quarterly analysis of the price/earnings ratio for private company sales in the UK (www.bdo.co.uk/pcpi) compared with public company P/Es for the same time period.

The reliability of P/E ratios

Theoretically the main factors determining a company's P/E ratio are its growth prospects and risk. The better the growth prospects then in theory the higher the P/E. On the other hand, the greater the risk, the lower the P/E.

In practice there is no consistent correlation between current earnings growth and share prices, or between risk and P/E ratios. The earnings figures of individual companies (and hence their P/Es) reflect their gearing and tax positions, and also their accounting policies. These discrepancies may be exacerbated in a period of inflation when earnings figures calculated on an historic cost basis will not be comparable. The main problems with quoted P/Es are threefold:

1 Dependence on share prices
2 Difficulties in finding truly comparable companies
3 Differences in capital structure

- **Dependence on share prices**. There are two points to bear in mind here:
  - General sentiment in the market can shift a company's price/earnings ratio dramatically and in the short term this may have little to do with long-term potential.
  - P/Es can be artificially high or low depending on where the comparable companies are in their reporting cycles or what the market thinks about future prospects. If a company's historic profits were low, but the market believes it will recover, price will remain relatively high, and with it the historic P/E, until the next set of results (or the next profit warning!) confirms or confounds market expectations

- **Difficulties in finding truly comparable companies**. As no two companies in the same sector operate in exactly the same way, with the same customer base, product range and geographic spread true comparisons are all but impossible. P/Es based on comparable companies must always, therefore, be seen as rough approximations

- **Differences in capital structure**. Earnings are calculated as shown in Figure 6.4

Fig 6.4	Calculating earnings
	£ million
Turnover, including related companies	2562.2
Less turnover of related companies	(442.7)
Turnover	2,119.5
Cost of sales	(1,086.3)
Gross profit	1,033.2
Distribution costs	(237.6)
Administrative expenses	(416.9)
Research and development	(46.8)
Share of profits of related companies	21.3
Income from other fixed asset investments	0.2
Operating profit	353.4
Interest (net)	(51.9)
Profit before tax	301.5
Tax on profit on ordinary activities	(82.9)
Profit on ordinary activities after tax	218.6
Minority interests	(13.4)
Earnings per 25p Ordinary Share, net basis (undiluted)	44.98p
Earnings per 25p Ordinary Share, net basis (fully diluted)	44.37p

Estimating sustainable earnings

It is not good enough just to take the target's earnings and use that without question. For all sorts of reasons the earnings figure might not be representative of the 'steady state'. Note that P/Es of comparable companies should be applied to an estimate of the *sustainable* earnings of the target'. Sustainable earnings to which the P/E ratio is applied should generally exclude exceptional items, interest on investments and cash balances not used in the business. For the acquisition of private companies in particular, the owner's benefits, which will not continue post-acquisition, need to be added back. Equally, costs not accounted for by the vendor in the past which have flattered profits need to be deducted to establish a more accurate picture.

When using P/Es to calculate the value of the target to the buyer, any synergy benefits need to be added to the target's stand-alone sustainable earnings.

All of this is easier said than done. Given that one of the main objectives of financial due diligence is to establish sustainable earnings, arriving at the sustainable earnings of the target company can involve a lot more than jotting a few numbers on the back of a cigarette packet.

All the above means that the determination of appropriate P/E ratios can be a complex task requiring many judgements and adjustments. Nevertheless, despite the limitations of P/Es in valuation, they are very widely used.

Other profit multiples

It really does not matter much which profit measure is used providing that all data are consistently either pre- or post-tax and pre- or post-amortisation and depreciation. In other words like has to be compared with like. Other popular multiples are:

EBIT	Earnings before Interest and Taxes
EBITDA	Earnings Before Interest, Tax, Depreciation and Amortisation
EBT (or PBT)	Earnings (Profit) before Tax

EBITDA has become a favourite over the last few years as the importance of operating cash flows in valuations has been recognised. EBITDA is profit before any financing costs and before charges for the largest non-cash items (Depreciation and Amortisation) and is seen as a good approximation to cash flow.

Profit multiples vs cash flow

Which is best? For M&A valuations there is no right answer to that question. Both techniques have their strengths and weaknesses and both should be used. As far as stock market valuations are concerned, however, the evidence suggests that the market values cash and can see through manipulations designed to increase reported earnings.[7]

4: Comparable transactions

As well as using comparable companies in P/E and profit multiple calculations, acquirers may also use comparable transactions as a benchmark on the not unreasonable grounds that a comparable transaction ought to be a good guide to the going rate for this type of company. This is fine if used with caution because sometimes companies are bought for strategic reasons and under these circumstances acquirers pay more than the going rate. However, if nothing else, comparable transactions can give buyers comfort that they are not paying too much.

5: Sector-specific valuation benchmarks

Publicly-quoted engineering companies are usually valued at around sales value. Similar norms exist in most industries. Table 6.2 gives a few examples of the benchmarks of value that might be used in a number of industries.

Table 6.2	Benchmarks of value
Industry / business	*Valuation benchmark*
Landfill	Price per cubic metre
Advertising agencies	Multiple of billings
Mobile telephone service	Price per subscriber
Cable TV	Price per subscriber
Fund managers	Multiple of funds under management
Hotels	Sale price per room
Mining companies	Value of mineral reserves
Professional firms	Multiple of fee income
Petrol retailers	Multiple of annual gallonage
Ready-mixed concrete	Price per cubic metre of output

6: Impact on earnings per share

A check on value popular amongst public companies is to gauge the acquisition's impact on pro-forma earnings per share. EPS dilution is not something to be tolerated. Of course there will only be dilution if one or all of the following apply:

- The target company is sizeable in comparison to the acquiring group
- The proposed purchase price values the target company at a significantly different earnings multiple than that of the acquirer
- The cost of overdraft or loan stock interest to finance the purchase will depress net earnings

The combined earnings-per-share figures should be calculated taking into account the overall impact of the acquisition including the effect of subsequent deferred payments to be made as part of an earn-out deal and the impact of the conversion of any convertible loan stock issued as purchase consideration.

7: Net asset backing

Net assets is a commonly-used basis for valuing small private companies, but it has serious drawbacks. The method is mostly reserved for valuing loss-makers or companies operating at break-even. The valuation of assets in a company's accounts is rarely useful in the context of an acquisition as:

- Historical cost figures are inadequate and current cost figures which might (in theory at least) be preferable are unlikely to be available
- Many significant assets may not be valued at all in the accounts – e.g. patents, designs, trademarks, brand names, copyrights, employees, customer lists and contracts. This is why businesses with a reasonable performance are likely to change hands at figures substantially higher than their book asset values
- Other assets (such as stock) can be overvalued in the accounts

A valuation based on the target's assets obviously needs a valuation of the assets. Expert valuations of land and buildings, stock and plant may be required and other balance sheet items may need careful investigation. The real value of work in progress, finished goods and debtors needs to be confirmed as they would in an audit and the adequacy of any provisions needs to be reviewed as does the extent of liabilities, including tax.

Conclusion

The soundest method for valuing acquisition targets is cash flow because it has fewer disadvantages than other methods and forces acquirers to quantify important assumptions. It is less subject to manipulation to produce a result in support of unsound thinking by company strategists. However, it still requires a number of simplifying assumptions which can have an impact on the calculation of value.

Because no one valuation method is perfect, it is best to use three different approaches. This allows the acquirer to 'triangulate' on value. It is also a good idea to work out the value of the business to the seller and to other possible bidders. A feel for both will help set the minimum and maximum acquisition prices that need be paid. A thorough and detailed calculation of synergies is vital in setting the maximum price that can be paid.

Notes

1 It obviously depends on the specifics of the transaction, but acquirers should expect to pay somewhere around 5–7 per cent of deal price in advisers' fees and there may be other transaction costs to add such as stamp duty.

2 Real options introduce a decision tree approach to Discounted Cash Flow (DCF) by recognising that the projection of cash flows should be made up of a number of decision nodes each with its own value and each with its own probability of occurring, and that the value of a company is the weighted average of this series of uncertain cash flows.

3 See for example Copeland, Tom, Koller, Tim and Murrin, Jack, *Valuation: Measuring and Managing the Value of Companies*, John Wiley & Sons, New York, 1990, Chapter 5.

4 Copeland *et al* (1990), p. 161.

5 Nominal is the number as it is, including inflation, real numbers have inflation excluded.

6 It is possible to take a PhD in the subject, such are its subtleties.

7 See for example Copeland *et al* (1990), pp. 81–94.

Negotiation 7

Good negotiating skills are an acquisition essential. At every step along the way, buyers and sellers find themselves negotiating over something. In the early days it will be over the indicative price, then it will be the Heads of Terms, next it will be the access for advisers carrying out due diligence and so on, until the Sale and Purchase Agreement is finally signed.

The high stakes and high pressure of M&A negotiations make careless mistakes easy and therefore the more you know, and the more you practise, the better you will be when it really counts.

The basics

As is implied by the title of one of the most famous books on the topic,[1] negotiation is about reaching agreement. No surprises there. The problem is that both sides are trying to reach a joint agreement starting from different points with different ideas on what they want. In most negotiations neither side actually has to settle, so coercion or large-scale trickery is really not going to work. The other side can simply walk away if it feels it is being manoeuvred into something unsuitable. Negotiation therefore involves persuasion. It also involves power and it is no good pretending otherwise. As President Nixon was fond of reminding us, 'when you have them by the balls their hearts and minds tend to follow'. The cooperative 'Getting to Yes' school of negotiation tends to brush this aside. But, as neither side has to reach agreement, the aim throughout should be an agreement which leaves both sides feeling positive about it. This is the 'win-win' of popular books on negotiation.

Win-lose is where all the excitement is and there is an argument with M&A negotiations which says because this is a one-off event and you do not have to work with the other side afterwards, screwing the other side is OK. There is some truth in this and we will look at the win-lose negotiating style later, but for now the important point to recognise is that 'win-win' is not the same as splitting the difference and it certainly does not mean both sides get the same thing. With 'win-win' the other side has to feel satisfied but perhaps not as satisfied as you.

Actions for a win-win negotiation are fairly straightforward. First make sure everyone understands. Signal clearly that your intentions are for a win-win negotiation and get confirmation from the other side that this is their position too. From there it is a question of avoiding as much conflict as possible until mutual trust has been established (if you bear in mind that the root of win-win is cooperative negotiation, all this makes much more sense). This means tackling the problems with the greatest potential for a win-win outcome first to get a good head of agreement steam going. Reinforce the sense of cooperation by sharing information, even if this is not initially reciprocated. Avoid a defensive posture. Avoid a legalistic or contractual approach and when you make a fool of yourself (which you will) quietly and firmly apologise and return the discussion to the subject of the negotiation.

However desperate you are to do the deal, disguise it. Watch the body language, play cool, be brisk and business-like. For this reason, although you may get the upper hand by choosing the venue – they have to come to you if it is in your offices – avoid lunch or any social aspect so that you do not have to play genial host.

The aim of successful negotiators is to avoid getting bogged down in bargaining over, or from, positions ('there is no way I am going to take the PCB dump as part of this deal', 'If you buy the company you take the people, the factory, the dump'). Interests are what are on the table and interests you must negotiate to get a deal. Positions are the Pretorian Guard of issues. It is a waste of time to try to knock them down. Go round them instead to reach a 'win-win' outcome. Appendix F gives a suggested checklist. To do this, of course, you have to have a clear picture of what the interests are on both sides. Which is why preparation is so important.

Preparation

One of the main reasons people fall down on negotiations is lack of preparation. We all have a tendency to 'wing it' and rely on our wits. Besides, preparing for a negotiation definitely comes under the 'too hard' heading. Hard it may be, but if you want to do well there is no escape. To be a good negotiator you have to be prepared to prepare.

The first thing to think about is about the procedure itself. Next be clear on what you want to achieve and, just as important, what is not acceptable. Finally set the walk-away point – be prepared to walk away if the deal is not right for you, this is also known as the 'BATNA' which is explained later in this chapter.

The procedure

Before you get into the detailed process of bargaining and compromise, draw up a list of things you need to establish with the other party. One of these should be the procedure for the negotiations themselves. Discuss this with the other parties with the objective of creating an environment for constructive negotiation.

For a Sale and Purchase negotiation, the core principles[2] might be that:

- There should be only one draft of the agreement prepared and negotiated
- The single text is to be prepared by lawyers from an independent law firm agreed upon by the parties and which has not represented any one of them in the past
- The first draft would be based on what the negotiators had already agreed
- The independent lawyers would be present at all negotiation sessions as observers, advisers, note-takers and, ultimately, drafters
- The only other people present at the negotiation sessions would be from the parties: business people, negotiators, in-house counsel
- External lawyers and other advisers would be excluded from the negotiation sessions. The parties would deal with them outside of the sessions
- Each negotiator would be fully empowered by his/her appointer to make decisions that would bind the appointer
- Venue to be your offices (preferably) or a neutral venue but never at their offices
- Everyone is working to an agreed and well-defined timetable

Interests

Negotiation is a process of trading. You will not negotiate successfully if you do not identify what your interests are: what are the needs, desires, concerns, and fears that have to be addressed in the negotiations?

Once identified, interests can be prioritised. The aim is to get to the point where you can say that unless certain interests are addressed to your satisfaction you are better off not entering into an agreement.

BATNA

This means developing real alternatives to entering into the agreement; alternatives that are achievable and that will meet your interests. Setting out the 'best alternative to a negotiated agreement', or BATNA as it is more commonly known, helps you focus because it tells you that there are alternatives, see Figure 7.1 below.

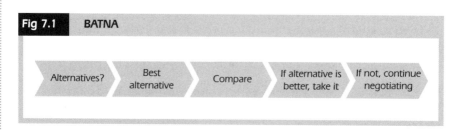

Fig 7.1   BATNA

Alternatives? → Best alternative → Compare → If alternative is better, take it → If not, continue negotiating

As the figure shows, BATNA is a way of structuring the decision on how far to go with negotiations. First list all the alternatives, and then look at the most promising in more detail (assuming all are practical propositions). Select the best of these and compare this with the alternative of continuing negotiations (and the compromises you are likely to make). If continuing negotiations is the best option then that is what you do. BATNA forces you to understand why you are doing the deal and gives you a pretty good idea of how strong your bargaining power is. The better your alternatives, the better your bargaining position. Think of this in personal terms. How much better do you think you would be at negotiating a pay rise with a job offer in your back pocket? If your bargaining position is not as strong as you would like, try to improve your BATNA before sitting down to negotiations.

Improving the BATNA – having the management in your pocket, literally
Barrie Pearson of Livingstone Guarantee tells a beautiful story of the time he sat down to discuss the management buyout of a people-dependent training and publishing business with a major multi-national having first secured, from the entire management team, letters of resignation if the buyout did not go ahead. Naturally these were in his inside pocket at the negotiating table.

Bargaining power is a relative concept. It is measured relative to your BATNA, but it is also measured against the other side's bargaining position. Having mapped out and prioritised your own interests do the same for the other side. Try to put yourselves in their shoes. Try to envisage what their interests are, what their alternatives are, and how the various matters can be dealt with in the final agreement. Solving the other side's problems is the best way of solving your own. As a negotiator, your job is to persuade the other side to say 'yes' to a proposal which meets your interests better than your no-deal option. For them to agree, your proposal must be better than their no-deal option. What you are trying to plan out is how to protect your interests, that is, how not to give too much away, by understanding where their interests lie and then persuading the other side that agreeing with you is in their best interests. It is the art of negotiation known as letting them have your way. Understanding where they are and building a bridge so they can reach your desired end point is much more effective than trying to push and shove the other side from its position to yours. Once you sit down to find out about the other side you will be surprised how much information there is out there.

Win-win and the overvalued maker of steel tube

When preparing to negotiate the acquisition of a specialist steel maker from a large public company, investigations revealed that it was valued in the current owners books at £40 m. This was a remarkably high number given its size and profitability. Further enquiries revealed that the public company had decided some years back that the tube maker would be sold and had therefore written up its book value to minimise capital gains on disposal. The potential acquirer would not pay anything like £40 m (more like £10 m in fact) and was the only serious game in town. A face saving formula had to be found whereby the present owner could claim a headline price of £40 m even though the actual price paid might be very different. An earn-out formula was devised which would pay £40 m in extreme and highly unlikely circumstances but would most likely lead to a price in the £10–£12 m range. Both sides came away happy.

From this you can map out various areas of interest, as in Table 7.1.

Table 7.1	Areas of interest	
Interest	*Type*	*Description / objective*
Mutual	Like	Interest that each party has and will want satisfying
Complementary	Different	Interests that each party has but which can be satisfied in a way that leaves everybody happy
Neutral	Different	Interests that cannot be satisfied without affecting the interests of the other party
Competing	Different	Interests that cannot be satisfied without affecting the interests of the other party

The map is used to think of options and packages that might be proposed. These options and packages are used to plan the negotiator's approach. The aim is to ensure that the negotiation flows so that mutual, complementary and neutral interests are addressed before competing interests.

Even for one-off negotiations building a relationship is the best way forward and dealing with the easiest areas first ensures an atmosphere of cooperation in which to address the competing interests.

Preparation on this scale means that you can think through your aspirations on each matter, with each aspiration grounded in reality, but set above the walk-away level.

Overall, the aim of the preparation is to go to the negotiating table:

- Knowing the mandate of the negotiator
- Knowing the walk-away points and having a good idea of where these lie for the other party
- Having improved the alternatives to a negotiated agreement (if at all possible)
- Knowing and having thought about your own interests
- Having thought about the interests of the other parties
- Having prepared mutually beneficial options and packages that could address competing interests

Knowledge is a major strategic weapon and these are really nothing more than the fundamentals – what is being negotiated, what your goals are, what your points to concede are. In addition, if you know your weak spot, it will be easier to conceal and if you can find the other side's, so much the better. Finally, good preparation minimises the risk of needing a piece of information on the spot and being unable to access it when the pressure is really on.

The negotiations

A negotiation is not a battle. The principles of good negotiating are:

- Each side shows concern for the other's objectives
- Each side sees the other as fair
- The outcome is win-win
- Each side feels it would enjoy negotiating again

The aim is to reach an agreement without leaving money on the table. In order to win the best from any negotiation, a blend of three important attributes is necessary:

- Skill
- Aspiration
- Power

Skill

Skill comes with practice, familiarity and watching others, but the more famil-iar you are with what makes a good negotiator, the better.

Good negotiators

There are a number of common characteristics which distinguish good negotia-tors. Good negotiators:

- Say very little but listen carefully
- Are not overtly aggressive
- Are shrewd
- Have ambitious goals (i.e. high aspirations)
- Never concede without gaining an advantage in return and then concede only slowly (see below under 'Trading concessions')
- Look for inexpensive concessions to trade for valuable ones
- Have influence and the ability to use it
- Have credibility and respect from the other side
- Have empathy for others
- Have agile minds and a capacity for sustained concentration. Negotiations always require quick thinking and the ability to concentrate on what is important
- Can think clearly under stress

Above all, they are characterised by the four Ps. They are:

- Patient
- Positive
- Placid
- Prepared

They also understand the rules of arguing, the dos and don'ts of which are out-lined in Table 7.2.

Table 7.2	The rules of arguing	
Do	*Do not*	
Make only a few points at a time – mention only a couple of the strongest points in your favour	Interrupt – you need to concentrate on picking up signals	
Demand point-by-point justification of the opposition's case	Provoke, say by raking up old disagreements	
Build up a case logically and carefully before drawing the conclusion that you disagree with the other side rather than the other way round. Saying you disagree and then why will only encourage the other side to argue point by point		
Check out their priorities		
Listen carefully and be positive		
Avoid point-scoring, uttering threats or anything else that will inevitably fan the flames		
Seek clarification of the other side's position through neutral summaries of what you understand their position to be		
Question – what areas are still open? What suggestions do the other side have? What, exactly, is the foundation of their case?		
Seek new variables – what else can be brought into the negotiations?		
Listen carefully – you need to concentrate on picking up signals		
Be positive – concentrate on how things can be improved		

Aspiration

The more successful party will usually be the one with the higher aspirations.[3] Aiming high means making high demands. While there is always the danger that high demands will turn the other side off, exaggerated demands can always be reduced and therefore they give headroom for making concessions.

When it looks like you are making concessions the other side will believe they are winning. Do not talk yourself down by being too anxious to please. The other side will chip away without help from you, so don't help them.

Power

Power is the capacity to influence the other person. There is always a link between power and results in negotiations. When one side has a strong power base, the differences in performance between skilled and unskilled negotiators become smaller. It is vital to build up a power base, whether it is real or apparent. A power base can be built up by having no real need to settle, little regard for the other side's status or power and personal confidence. Aiming high means behaving as if you have power. Indeed negotiations can often be influenced if the other side merely believes you have power. First impressions are particularly important and are aided by both building up a logical argument and by relaxing and avoiding over-aggression. In other words, power and confidence go hand-in-hand, underlining once again the fact that negotiations need to be well-prepared and well-planned.

However, power is easily abused. Be sure that weaker parties are not frightened away from the negotiating table thus leading to a lose-lose outcome. The movies may be full of tough guy negotiators bulldozing the other side to get the lion's share of the spoils but real life negotiations are 50 per cent emotion and if the other side thinks it is being bounced into something which is unfair, damages its reputation or damages its self-esteem, it is much more likely to call the whole thing off even if it is economically irrational.

At the other end of the power spectrum:

- Do not negotiate when you have nothing to bargain with, or when broader objectives might be prejudiced
- Do not be caught ill-prepared by having to do quick deals

Assess the other side's power base. It will usually be overestimated, so try to verify it in the preparatory phase. This observation leads on to a much wider principle which should always be borne in mind. Perceptions are everything and what you really need to understand are your opponents' perceptions. Get inside your opponents' head. The really expert negotiator is the one who mentally sits in the chair opposite.

Starting discussions

Where do you start? Unless there is a really big issue which if not resolved will mean no deal, start with points that are likely to bring the two sides together. This serves two purposes:

- As already mentioned, it is the 'getting to know you' stage
- It allows you to gather information. You can use this stage to find out what is motivating them in order to gauge their real needs rather than their desires. You should also assume that the same tactic is being used on you so do not give too much away!

It pays to concentrate initially on building a working relationship. People negotiate better with someone they trust. Negotiation is a highly sophisticated form of communication. Without trust, there will be no communication but instead manipulation and suspicion masquerading as communication. Be trustworthy. Honour your commitments. Tell the truth. Respect confidences. Make sure your word is your bond. If you do not show trustworthiness and commitment, why should the other side?

Language (and body language which we will come to later) is very important in building a relationship. For example it is not a good idea not to counter the other side's proposals by openly disagreeing. 'I see what you are saying, but…' is not a great opening. Much better is 'I understand your point of view and…' because you are being inclusive, constructive and building on their foundations. Do not just say 'no' when rejecting suggestions from the other side. Explain why so that the other side can find alternatives. Be sparing with the word 'but' as it signals a negative approach. Get the negotiations back into a positive frame by asking directly about the other party's concerns (having spotted the 'but' as a sign that they have concerns) and address those concerns positively.

However, this is not just a cosy chat. Your job is to get the other side to agree on terms which are favourable to you, so do not forget some of the old salesmen's tricks such as asking, 'where will you put the sofa Mrs X?', thus planting the idea in the head of the would-be house purchaser that the deal will be done. You can also try the old double-glazing salesman's trick of manoeuvring your questions so that the other party can only say 'yes' to you. The more they become accustomed to agreeing with you, the smoother the negotiations will be. Both approaches also have the advantage of keeping the other side relaxed and therefore likely to give more away.

Of course these tactics will be played on you too so watch for 'yes' tags such as 'don't you agree?'. Become a fly on the wall so you can assess what is truly going on. If the 'yes' tactic is worked on you, always qualify your 'yes': 'yes, providing…'.

Ask questions...listen to the answers

Nor is negotiation about fast talking. When talking, be relaxed and fluent but above all learn to shut up and listen. No matter how well you have prepared, you will not know everything about the other side's interests. Always question what the other side really wants and probe for this. Always try to find, so that you can exploit, the other person's fears. These will be a mix of:

- Emotional
- Personal
- Objective i.e. fear of not getting certain points agreed
- Fears may be based around losing face, or undermining relationships with colleagues
- Other people
- Being inadequate

To confirm the interests and fears of the other side, ask questions. Questions will have to be a bit more subtle than simply 'what's your worst nightmare about this?', but ask lots of them and listen. Where do they stumble and stutter? The inexperienced negotiators are the ones who do not listen. Listen not just to the words but also to what is being said. Also observe and watch the body language. Above all, do not be forever thinking about what you are going to say next.

Do remember, though, that there are cultural differences as to what questions can be asked and in what way. Direct open questions are fine for Americans but not for Japanese. Remember also that the message may not always be 'up-front'. It will with Americans but not with the Japanese.

As the discussions proceed, move from non-directed, open questions to more specific questions on the broad issues and watch the responses very carefully. Do they try to sidestep you? If so, try again but be even more direct – but without being aggressive. Watch the body language while you do this. If they are still sidestepping take note of the question. This is obviously a sensitive topic. Then you either:

- Back off and approach the same issue a little later from a different direction, or
- Imply that you already know the answer – so there is no point them holding out, or
- Use silence. Ask the question and simply keep quiet until it is answered

Use silence

Listening produces silence. Silence can be a very effective negotiating tool. Do not feel the need to fill the gaps (most people do). Ask the question and shut up. Make the proposal and shut up. Wait for the other side to respond until you speak again. Silence is a frighteningly powerful weapon which can force the other side to expand on their statements and sometimes to modify them. How many times have you seen TV reporters use it to great effect? Use silence as well to counter incomplete or dubious statements. Silence with raised eyelids and a slight raising of the eyebrows is a real killer.

Answering their questions

Both sides will be digging all the time, using questions to uncover the other side's thinking. Many questions will be loaded, 'when did you stop beating your wife?' type questions. The best ploy is to answer them in a straightforward way: 'People always ask me when I last beat my wife. That is a loaded question because they probably already know the answer. I'd also like to point out that some things, like domestic matters and our discussions here today, should be kept confidential. I am sure you do not want me to tell the world about the deal we are negotiating'.

Otherwise question the question but without too much aggression. You are trying to dismiss its relevance, not undermine the questioner: 'why does my wife have any bearing on these negotiations?' Tony Blair used to use this technique very effectively with Ian Duncan Smith. Duncan Smith would ask a question and Blair would reply along the lines of, 'Of all the questions he could have asked, it should not have been this one'. The result was to get Blair off the hook and sound helpful and reasonable at the same time.

Of course when the boot is on the other foot, you want full answers to all your questions before moving on.

Keeping control

A lot of the stresses in negotiating come from the feeling that you are out of control. We will turn to some of the more obvious stress-inducing manoeuvres in a moment but remember establishing and keeping control of the negotiations can make all the difference so be the one to take the chair and be the one to sum up. Taking the initiative will not only help you, it will also gain you the respect of the other side.

Keep the plates spinning but be aware of unnecessary ones designed to bring you down and do not be afraid to ask for clarification or a recap of point agreed if things seem to be going too fast for your liking. Besides clarifying what has been agreed so far, this is a good way of slowing things down and breaking the other side's momentum. Summarise regularly, and feel free to suggest a recess when you need time to plot your further course. Always:

- Keep notes
- Keep cool
- Step back from time to time

Dealing with tactical ploys

Aggression

The problem with aggression is that it kicks in the ancient fight or flight response. Be assertive but not aggressive. Assertion is getting your point across. Whatever happens, stay calm and get your point across.

If negotiations become heated and personal do not fight fire with fire. Maintain your position as an adult even in the face of outrageous provocation. The more heated they become the cooler you become. Use very long silences after verbal attacks to emphasise their stupidity. Make no reference to the attacks when you do eventually speak. Get back to the issue – and watch for any information the outburst may reveal.

If the other side is ranting and raving it is using more energy than you so will flag first. Just wait. Simply restate your position from time to time. Do not take aggression personally – it is a tactic. Continue to treat the other side exactly how you would wish to be treated.

Non-aggression

At the opposite end of the scale, beware of nice negotiators. Do not let them lull you into lowering your guard and giving too much away. Do not think you do not need to prepare properly because the other side is 'nice'.

Anger

Anger must be used sparingly otherwise the negotiator will lose control. It is best deployed to counter an outrageous suggestion from the other side – and it can be very effective if it gets the message across that one side cannot continue to treat the other like this.

151

Emotion

Emotion can be used very effectively provided it is kept under control. As soon as a negotiator loses their temper they have given away control of the negotiation. However, the whole gamut of emotion can, should be and is used to put a message across. Culture often determines how much emotion can be used.

Experts

Experts are sometimes used to shift the balance of power. Always ask beforehand who will be present at any negotiation and their role. If a technical expert subsequently turns up, sidestep him or her by asking that things be put in writing so that you can get your technical experts to answer. On no account try to negotiate.

> The financial controller was a power in the land and used to getting his own way. When the joint venture in which his company was a minority partner came up with a well-researched and logical acquisition proposal, which his chairman did not want to happen, he asked his contacts at a leading City investment bank to come up with their opinion as to an appropriate discount rate to use in the DCF calculations. Of course this was outrageously high and made the proposed target look ridiculously expensive. The business development director in the joint venture was able to play exactly the same game and asked a similarly respected investment bank for its opinion. Its rate was close to the one used in the original paper and made the target look like a good buy. 'The only surprise is that he didn't fire me on the spot', said the business development director soon afterwards, 'but it was a stupid stunt. If he didn't want to do the deal, why didn't he just say so instead of trying to discredit it?'

Threats

Veiled threats along the lines of, 'there will be dire consequences if you don't do this deal' are either the stronger party hoping to gain an advantage or the weaker one hoping to hide weakness. Expose the threat by asking for clarification. Show that threats do not bother you: 'do what you will but our view remains that ...'.

An ultimatum

An ultimatum should only be used as a last resort. The weakness of the ploy is that it is often played too soon. Thus if someone plays the card against you, immediately make them think they are deploying it too early.

Lies

Do not assume everyone is entirely honest all of the time. It would be surprising if any negotiator ever was. Do not take everything at face value but do not tolerate out-and-out lies either. There cannot be serious negotiations if one side is lying. If you suspect the other side, first of all watch for tell-tale signs in their body language – hand over mouth, eye pull, ear pull, restricted movements. Then listen carefully to the content of what they are saying. A tangled web is difficult to weave successfully. Take regular breaks to review the information and ask for proof of their suspicious-sounding statements. All the time give them the opportunity to save face but if all fails, just leave.

Feigned misunderstanding

A frequently used ploy is pretending to have misunderstood a point already agreed. This is done for one of five reasons:

- To concede it to keep negotiations going
- To slow things down
- To retract a point already conceded without losing face
- To buy time
- To gain a concession

Good cop/bad cop

Another frequently-used tactic is to have a 'goodie' and 'baddie' on the other side's negotiating team. The theory is that if the baddie does not wear you down you will be so relieved when the goodie takes over the negotiations you will concede almost anything. Of course you will not! What you will do is put a stop to it by:

- Telling the other side it has been rumbled, 'Oh no, not the old good cop/bad cop routine. Can we grow up and get down to some proper negotiations?' might be a bit strong – after all, you do not want to embarrass them. 'I can't negotiate when there are two quite distinct positions' might be better

153

- Cutting out the hard man. A subsidiary of a Fortune 500 company was buying a small business run by two entrepreneurs. The big company man handled the negotiations on his own and was rightly also thinking about how to integrate the business afterwards. However he found himself in confrontational discussions about price and the deal with one of the sellers and then in consensus-driven discussions with the other one about how to work together in the new world. Of course the two entrepreneurs were liaising and manipulating the big company man, who tied himself up in knots and traded unnecessary concessions. He should have had a partner so the sides were more matched, instead of going it alone and trying to get a feather in his cap.
- Explain to the friendly one that you can't go on if the other one continues to play a part in the negotiations

Bluff and deception

If someone says something with enough confidence there is a pretty good chance it will be believed, especially if said from a position of authority. Take everything with a pinch of salt. Verify and question and watch for inconsistencies because, like lies, misinformation is difficult to maintain.

Option limitation

A very effective tactic is the use of blanket statements that close off options completely. Always question them. Some of history's greatest leaders have relied on just such a tactic to build their arguments. Stalin, for example, was prone to using phrases like 'it is true that' or 'it is axiomatic that' when nothing could have been further from the truth or less axiomatic. If the other side comes up with reasons like 'it is company policy', look them in the eye and ask when the policy was set and by whom. If it is claimed that there is 'only so much left in the budget', ask 'When are budgets set? When will there be a new allocation?'. If the response to your very reasonable offer of a trade is 'I'll have to refer', who is the person who makes the decisions and can you speak to him or her?

In a similar vein, precedent is often used as an excuse, 'we always do it that way, we can't change now'. The answer is that this is a unique negotiation, times change, and negotiating could give a better outcome than precedent.

Another variation is the other side saying 'I am sorry but...' followed by 'this is beyond my authority/I need to get approval from the boss/etc'. Take a good hard look at the excuse as it could be a bluff. If you think it is a bluff call it in the subtlest way you can.

The non-negotiable item

This is a form of option limitation. In fact, there is no such thing. Everything has a value and all values are relative. When confronted with something 'non-negotiable', show that it troubles you and either:

- Try to prise it open, 'so if we meet all your aspirations on price and warranties, you will still want to keep the Wimbledon debentures?', or

- Set it aside. Move onto other topics where you know you can reach agreement in order to create a sense of momentum and achievement

However the negotiations subsequently go, make sure you exact a steep price for the other side's intransigence – even if the non-negotiable item has a low value for you. After all, by billing it as non-negotiable the other side is basically saying 'this is worth a lot to me' and should therefore be prepared to trade a lot in order to secure it.

Blinded by science

Do not be blinded by science or numbers. Make sure you understand. Of course you will be properly prepared so documents will be readily to hand, won't they?

Bluff

Bluff only if you are prepared to have it called.

Trading concessions

Trading concessions is the core of the negotiating process. The golden rules are always:

- Trade, never concede
- Remember that the philosophy underpinning negotiation is normally 'win-win'
- Keep things in perspective. Know what the important issues are and concentrate on winning them. Your aim is to win the war
- Reward positive signals from the other side – frequency of concession counts for a lot more than size of concession
- Give concessions you do not mind losing. Although there must be give-and-take, try to take more than you give as far as your own values are concerned, that is, always trade something that is worth more to the other side than it is to you. The win-win comes if your minor points are the other side's major points and *vice versa*

- Your concessions should be small and tentative, but regular, in order to encourage the other side to respond
- Remember the other side will be doing exactly the same, presenting concessions in a way which is attractive to you but will be looking for something which is favourable to it. The key to all successful negotiations is seeing what lies behind the positioning
- Accept concessions grudgingly and minimise their value to you
- When you concede, make your opponent feel that you have given up something which you really value
- Be alive to other trades that might enhance your position. Sometimes there is an opportunity to get something even bigger: 'If we are doing that surely it makes sense also to do this'
- Look for opportunities to link one concession to another
- Look out for trump cards. A trump card is something you have that isn't worth much to you but is worth loads to the opposition. Explain in the negotiations that you couldn't possibly satisfy it. Show reluctance to discuss further. Gain a hypothetical concession in the unlikely event that you can fulfil it. Try to gain agreement to all your remaining objectives. Play the trump card
- Remember, there is nothing you want at any price

Case study 7.1 The art of making concessions really count

People like to win. Some negotiators will even count concessions won. Give them the opportunity to score by making suggestions you don't mind being knocked down from – with the aim of course of making your preferred choice the compromise option. This assists the win-win. Make it look like you are abandoning cherished principles and the concession will count for even more in the eyes of the other side.

The soon-to-retire sales director of a well-known forklift distributor was summarising his accumulated wisdom after more than forty years in forklift sales. 'The average member of the purchasing department' he said, 'wants a discount. If he got 10 per cent off list price last year, he wants 15 per cent this year. He can then go to his boss and report a victory. Never mind that we can manipulate the list prices and that he could get much better net prices if he tried. My tactic, of course, has always been to give him exactly what he wants, providing I get something in return like an extra spares contract – but I will make sure he works for it. I'll stay all day if I have to. At the end of a day's bargaining he feels so much better for having made me back down from what at 9.00 am was non-negotiable that he forgets about the fact that he will actually be paying out more than they did last year.'

Splitting the difference

Never offer to split the difference early on. It is a sign that you are not comfortable entering into a lengthy negotiation. Splitting the difference only makes sense at the end and then when the difference is small. When you split the difference, emphasise the sacrifice you have made.

Dealing with pressure devices

Pressure devices are an extreme tactical ploy designed to bounce or scare the other side into an agreement.

Time

Again a favourite of the double-glazing salesman for example 'we can offer you this deal but will have to agree now'. The effect is that the buyer usually slams on the brakes. This is absolutely the right thing to do. Do not allow yourself to be rushed. Much of the 'high pressure' of high-pressure salesmanship is in fact a form of bullying. If this is a good deal (for you), why must it be done in such a hurry?

From your perspective, making your opponent sweat a little may at times be appropriate. If they are pressurising you with deadlines, for example, putting the deal in doubt may be the best way of regaining the upper hand. Whatever, the aim is to seize the initiative and put pressure on them. You hope to distract them from the key issues and make them focus on just getting the deal done. Tactics you might use include:

- Playing the reluctant buyer/seller
- Creating your own 'higher authority' as a stumbling block
- Suspending negotiations altogether
- Withdrawing an offer already proposed
- Creating the impression that their tactics have caused you to lose heart and that you see little point in continuing

The fake stalemate

There will always be one. It is another pressure device. Do not start conceding to keep the deal on the table. When they ask for your suggestions on how to keep things moving, the answer is a question, 'I'm not sure, what do you suggest?' With any luck they will respond with solutions and the whole thing will be back on again. Or they will realise what you are up to and respond in kind. Trench warfare will ensue, which is no good for either side. Instead let them believe that they are the better more experienced negotiator by getting them to tell you what needs to happen next, something like, 'We would really like to find a way to do this deal but not at this price. What would that way be?' If it is a fake stalemate the other side will normally respond. If no concession is made there really is not much point negotiating further unless you change your position, so either do that or leave. If you leave, leave the door open for them to come back to you with a solution.

Last-minute changes

You know the story. After weeks of hard work, late nights and worry the deal is finally in sight when the other side pops up with a last-minute change: 'we cannot agree unless we get b, c and d'. It is funny how this seemingly now vital condition has not been mentioned once in the preceding negotiations. Goalposts changing right at the end may well be a bluff. Do not bluntly call it because doing so is tantamount to calling the other side liars. Stay cool and in control, appear to go along with the new circumstances but expose the disadvantages to them of changing the deal.

From your perspective, there is nothing wrong with using afterthought as a lever. Agreements are reached on a package. If a deal is stacking up well it will gather its own momentum. Furthermore, a lot of time will have been invested. A point late in the negotiations, when all looks to be heading for a successful conclusion, can be a good time to introduce something you want. Agreement is much more likely if it looks like everything achieved so far will be wasted without it.

Unblocking bottlenecks

Deadlock might seem uncomfortable but is perfectly normal and anyway there is not much you can do about it immediately so relax and enjoy it! The party which offers the first concession will usually be the less successful, so delight in doing nothing for a while.

Having, of course, predetermined your fallback position, you are going to stick to it. The other side will normally offer alternatives. All new offers should be treated as fresh negotiations and beware of the counter offer that is actually totally different from the original offer.

If you want to try breaking the deadlock try the following:

- Look for a new angle. Try to find new ideas based on the other side's real wants
- Take a break from formal negotiations and talk informally
- Create a diversion – change emphasis, location or people
- Make a (reluctant) offer of an unwanted concession
- Suggest a trade-off of a concession already agreed
- Propose a recess
- Restate and clarify both sides' positions showing areas of agreement and barriers to progress
- Trade minor concessions for a major move in your direction

Then consider the following:

- Issue a deadline
- Get them to put their cards on the table – how keen are they really? What are their most and least important concerns?
- Shame them. Ask straight up why all these meetings and no progress, then propose an alternative schedule
- Put them on the defensive with some heavyweight demands. That should reveal their true hand
- Show the other side you are in no rush and can live without this deal

If all this fails, the next step is getting up and walking away. It is a powerful tactic and widely used. Don't use it:

- Until you have tried everything else you know
- If you believe there is still a chance of reaching an amicable agreement
- Unless you have calculated your alternatives and know you can afford to walk out
- Unless you are prepared to have your bluff called and lose everything

But if then the other side will not budge, get up and go. Do not make it confrontational and do not burn bridges. Leave the door open for negotiations to restart.

Body language

Body language is very important. It makes up 55 per cent of all communication and is therefore well worth understanding.

Open

An open posture involves standing or sitting with the body facing the other person, hands palm up and on show, head lifted in interest, eyes open, legs and arms uncrossed. It indicates:

- A willingness to listen
- A feeling of strength
- Openness of mind
- Possessiveness

Closed

A closed posture involves standing or sitting with the body away from the other person, hands palm down or hidden from view, head down and eyes partly closed or constantly looking away. It indicates:

- A defensive attitude
- A negative attitude
- An unwillingness to change mind, thought or position

Leg crossing

Facing someone, crossed legs are defensive and negative. Sitting next to someone if they cross their legs towards you indicates that they are comfortable in your presence and are willing to engage in conversation. If they cross them away it says the opposite.

Leaning

Leaning towards another person and entering their space indicates a willingness to be closer in mind to that person. But too close and it becomes threatening. Use 'towards' positioning to indicate a willingness to change. Leaning away means you are trying to distance yourself from their point of view.

Eyes

The position of the upper eyelid relative to the iris tells all. The higher the upper eyelid, the higher the interest. If you can see the white above the pupil it indicates that the other person is experiencing shock or surprise. When the eyelid is between the top of the iris and the pupil it indicates a high level of interest. If the upper eyelid is level with the centre of the pupil, interest is flagging and when it has fallen below the pupil it indicates boredom.

The green light

All the sales books put emphasis on testing for the green light. Do not miss the signal to agree and continue negotiating. The green light is the finishing line – you can stop. Spotting the green light is a matter of spotting when the negotiator starts to relax. When they are thrashing through the negotiations their mind is working hard. Their body will be alert and upright to reflect this. As soon as they have made a decision their minds will slow down and their bodies will relax as well. Test for the green light by asking for agreement to take the deal onto the next stage. Then say nothing. Add anything more at this stage and you will only end up conceding more than you need to reach an agreement.

Learn to recognise and return signals

Signals are a vital part of negotiating, whether you are giving them or receiving them. They can indicate the style of negotiation, what you (and the other side's) needs are, degrees of commitment and areas for profitable exploration. Beware of giving unintentional signals.

Open gestures say the other side is at ease with what you are proposing. 'Towards' motions are a sign that you have raised a point of interest. Jump in quick with an open question to understand what interests them and why.

Signals should not be ignored, unless they are false. When received they should be explored.

What to do when 'win-win' will not work

The default option should be to seek a win-win outcome, so that both sides can obtain the best overall result. However, if the other side goes for a win-lose outcome you should also revert to an aggressive, competitive, win-lose approach.

The cooperative approach will just not work in such circumstances as it requires both sides to negotiate. Similarly, there may be times when you feel just so over-whelmingly powerful that 'win-win' is unnecessary.

Win-lose tactics

A win-lose attempt against you must be resisted and, if possible, penalised, to protect future negotiations. After that to defend against win-lose:

- Dig in early and present clear, but unemotional, opposition
- Exhibit rock-solid confidence
- Keep a balanced and detached view
- Keep control of what you are prepared to discuss and in what order
- Monitor carefully the pace and atmosphere of the discussion. Be prepared to redirect it if necessary
- Avoid initially either an aggressive stance or, for that matter, a defensive one. Both can be a stimulus to fighting
- Seek an exchange of information to clarify each side's position
- Stress the consequences to the other side of failing to resolve the issue. The intention here is to enhance mutual respect, while indicating quite clearly the predicament both sides will be in if they fail to agree
- Try to set up a shared problem-solving mechanism to move the other party to a win-win stance

Win-lose, being competitive, may be preferable where you know for sure you can win a power struggle. To succeed in a win-lose against another party:

- Make clear your absolute commitment to what you must have
- State what the consequences will be if you don't get it
- Try to prevent your opponents from specifying their commitments. If they do, provide some sort of face-saving exit for them
- Your objective is to convince the other side that the best outcome you could accept is the least you can possibly expect. However, it is a negotiation so you will have to trade concessions. The skill is slowly and painfully giving small concessions in exchange for big ones
- If you find yourself on difficult ground, be prepared to be flexible by chang-ing topic or tactics

Conclusion

Negotiation is concerned with resolving conflict usually by trading concessions. Trust, not trickery, is an important requirement for successful negotiation. Negotiation does not always have to imply confrontation, although it may sometimes require an element of brinkmanship, which is why skilled negotiators conclude better deals. Nevertheless, sustainable results are more often reached when all parties perceive the process as straightforward and fair. Plan as thoroughly as you possibly can:

- Establish your aims
  - What are the key aims?
  - What relative values do you place on them?
  - What is your negotiating range?
- Get information about the opposition
  - Answer the above from the other side's point of view

Remember negotiation needs both intuition and logic. Logic by itself produces the out-of-control spirals seen when computers trade shares. In such instances, intuition would say there must be bargains to be had in big sell offs. Plans are a support only – there are times when you may need to ignore plans despite the effort that has gone into them. It is a bit like having a shopping list but still wanting to take advantage of the 2-for-1 bargains. You have to be sensitive to the moment but on the other hand too much intuition means that decisions are taken too quickly. However, negotiations take place in real time so a skilled negotiator has to be able to go with the flow and trust instincts. The subconscious will have picked up what the conscious has missed – body language, tone of voice etc. Try to access the subconscious by self-questioning. If it feels wrong it probably is. Practice makes perfect and good negotiation skills are transferable. Watch other people negotiating and learn from them.

- Reach for compromise
- Try to give them what they value and you do not, **and**
- Gain what you value and they do not, **but**
- There will be issues which are important to both sides

Notes

1 Fisher, Roger and Ury, William, *Getting to Yes*, Random House, London, 1999.

2 Based on an article by Dr. K.C. Mildwaters in the AMR Management Bulletin, March 2000.

3 Thorn, Jeremy G., *How to Negotiate Better Deals*, Mercury Business Paperbacks, London, 1989.

The sale and purchase agreement

8

The confidentiality agreement was signed long ago, the letter of intent is a distant memory and the due diligence is over. Both parties should now be sufficiently informed to negotiate a definite acquisition agreement. In Common Law jurisdictions these agreements are fairly lengthy. The lawyers point out that they have to deal with the many eventualities which reflect the due diligence and evaluations which have proceeded it.

The party which draws up the first draft is normally at a negotiating advantage as the first draft sets the tone, style and structure of the agreement. Furthermore, there is a good chance that the other side will confine itself to criticising what is written rather than introducing new ideas. It is best to be even-handed rather than annoy the other side with a blatantly one-sided first draft. However, there is nothing wrong with introducing the odd clause you know will be deleted so that the other side can be lulled into thinking it has scored when you reluctantly concede a few points.

Why is a contract necessary?

The shares in a company can be transferred from one person to another with a single-page stock transfer form bought from any legal stationer. Why go to the bother of preparing a share sale and purchase agreement of anything up to 200 pages? The answer is that when a company is purchased through a share sale, it comes together with all its assets and liabilities irrespective of whether the buyer actually wants them. In a company with a long history or a company which has traded extensively this may involve a buyer picking up historical, unknown and unquantified liabilities. A share sale and purchase agreement therefore introduces certainty for both sides by enabling a buyer to know that it is buying exactly what it thinks it is buying and enabling a seller to sell exactly what it wants to sell. It also gives the buyer some legal protection should the business not be in the state that it thought.

In the Anglo-Saxon jurisdictions, the acquisition of shares is governed by the law of contract. Neither party is obliged to disclose facts to the other. This explains why purchasers make extensive enquiries about the company and put a provision in the contract to say that it has relied on the vendors' answers. The acquirer should find out everything it needs to know about an acquisition target before completing the transaction. But what if the seller does not tell the acquirer the truth or does not tell the acquirer the whole story in response to questions? Or what if there are some questions to which it is impossible to have a definite answer before the transaction completes? The contract will contain negotiated provisions, known as warranties and indemnities, to deal with both these eventualities. In addition, there are two legal reasons why the acquirer needs to consider specific legal protection when buying a company:

- Under English law, the acquirer buys a company on a 'goods as seen' basis and trying to get a refund is no fun! In Latin this is the *caveat emptor* or 'buyer beware' principle
- Acquirers cannot rely on the audited accounts of the target company. If those accounts have been negligently audited, an acquirer can only hope to sue the auditors in the most exceptional circumstances

In contrast, with an asset sale the buyer only purchases those assets it wants and leaves behind anything it does not want.

The agreement

Basically, the acquisition agreement should set out:

- The principal financial terms of the transaction, and
- The structure of the transaction

The acquisition agreement will also include:

- The legal rights and obligations of the parties
- The remedies for breaches of these obligations
- The actions that the parties must take prior to completion of the transaction

The agreement should form a comprehensive record of the entire agreement between the parties on all aspects of the transaction. This reduces the possibility of future arguments. To do this, it needs to set out clearly who is buying what, when they are buying it, for how much and on what terms. It also needs to state that it represents the entire agreement between the parties.

The agreement should set out the immediate changes which need making to the target company. These will include matters such as the resignation and appointment of directors, the resignation and appointment of auditors, the repayment of bank debt and changes to the constitution of the company.

The traditional order of the agreement's sections are:

- Commencement
- Recitals
- Deal points
- Representations and warranties
- Restrictive covenants
- Definitions
- Conditions to closing
- Indemnification
- General

Commencement

The commencement section has two main points:

Formalities for execution

In some European countries, but by no means all, special conditions must be met before an agreement can come into force. Under German law, for example, agreements must be notarised to be enforceable. This means all documents that form the transaction must be notarised. In Holland only the transfer of shares needs notarisation.

The parties

Clearly the agreement should list the parties, but sometimes it is not that obvious who they are. Only the shareholders on either side can make the agreement work but there may be complications. If there are trustees, the trustees must be involved from the beginning and the powers of the vendor director/vendor shareholder must be checked very carefully. Very often, for example, the terms of the trust will prevent trustees from giving warranties. This will knock a hole in the timetable if the warranties given by a vendor director/shareholder are assumed to have been given on behalf of all shareholders.

Recitals

These are the paragraphs which describe (i.e. recite) the reasons for the agreement or the background against which the agreement should be read. Confusingly, these paragraphs begin with the word 'whereas'.

Deal points

The initial section of the acquisition agreement traditionally contains the deal points. The deal points typically explain the precise mechanics for transferring the shares and any underlying companies to the buyer and when and how the purchase price is to be calculated and paid.

Type of consideration

Although there are many variations, there are three basic ways in which the buyer can meet the purchase price:

- Cash
- Shares
- Debt

Cash

This is largely self-explanatory. Cash is normally acceptable to sellers subject to tax considerations.

Shares

Shares can take many forms including ordinary shares, preference shares, convertible shares and redeemable shares.[1] Sellers taking shares as payment will consider very carefully all of the rights attaching to the shares and whether the value is, or will be, enough to meet the price. For instance:

- How and when are dividends payable?
- Is a fixed dividend payable and what happens if dividends are not paid?
- Is there a market for the shares if the seller wishes to sell them and will that be permitted under the articles of association of the company?
- Are there effective controls against transactions draining value out of the buying company whilst the seller holds shares in it?
- What protections are there against the buyer diluting shareholdings?

Debt

The main issues the seller will consider are:

- Rate of interest – fixed or variable?
- Does the rate of interest reflect the risk that is being taken by the seller in accepting debt?
- What is the creditworthiness of the issuer and should a guarantee be obtained from a parent company or bank?

- What are the events of default which will make the debt repayable in full?
- Is the debt transferable?

Guarantee of the guarantee

As far as the seller is concerned, the buyer should guarantee payment of the agreed price when the agreement is signed, unless some sort of deferred consideration has been agreed. Usually the seller is not satisfied with the simple signature of the agreement by the buyer, and asks for a 'guarantee of the guarantee'. In this case, the most common form of guarantee is the commitment of a financial institution to pay the amount due by the buyer if the latter does not.

Timing of the consideration

The consideration could be for a fixed amount payable at completion, or for an initial element with additional tranches payable subsequently depending on, say, performance or the absence of warranty claims or following satisfactory completion accounts. The concept of consideration being dependent on future performance can raise difficulties because post-completion performance will be to some extent dependent on the new owners. Consideration related to post-completion performance is, therefore, best kept to short-term events such as making it dependent on the state of the company at completion.

Retentions

A retention is when the buyer holds back part of the consideration. Retentions are used primarily where the buyer is concerned about the future creditworthiness of the seller to give comfort that warranty and indemnity claims will be met. The buyer holds back some of the purchase consideration which can then be set off against claims under the warranties or indemnities. They are also used when the seller undertakes to deliver something after the deal, such as the consent of a major supplier to a change of control or hitting a particular profit figure.

The main issues to address with retentions are:

- Why is the retention being used? It is important that the reason is clear in the agreement
- Who will hold the retention? Who is responsible for releasing it? Where will it be held and what type of account will be used?
- What happens to the retention monies and any interest earned on them? The usual terms are that the party to whom payment is made also gets the interest
- The circumstances under which the retention will be released

Escrow

The use of a retention avoids the buyer taking a risk on the seller's creditworthiness if there is a claim. In order to avoid the seller taking on the risk that the buyer will not pay over any retentions in the future if they are not used, money is usually paid into an escrow account. An escrow account is nothing more than a bank account opened in the joint names of the solicitors representing the buyer and the seller. The money is only released when the agreed requirements are met. If they are not, the money is repaid to the buyer.

Table 8.1 sets out how the main M&A risks can be addressed using escrow accounts:[2]

Table 8.1	M&A risks and escrow solutions
Risks	*Escrow solutions*
For the buyer	**Buyer protection**
The representations and warranties made by the seller are untrue.	A proportion of the purchase price is put in an escrow account for a specified time. If in that time the representations and warranties do turn out to be untrue the escrow funds can be turned over to the buyer.
Covenants (see below) agreed by the seller are not honoured.	As above.
There are key employees in the business who may leave.	Cash or shares are placed in escrow to be released over time if the employee remains.
A seller cannot or will not pay advisers' fees.	Advisers' fees are paid into escrow and released when the advisers' work is complete.
For the seller	**Seller protection**
The buyer does not pay up on earn-outs.	Earn-out premiums are placed in escrow and paid over to the seller once performance benchmarks are reached.
For both parties	**Protection**
Approvals, e.g. from government, are not forthcoming.	Both the consideration and the shares are placed in escrow and only passed over once approval is forthcoming.

As a matter of practice it is important that the escrow instructions (which may need to be carried out some time after the agreement is signed) are clear on all of the above matters and in particular give precise instructions about when the money can be released and to whom.

Earn-outs

Earn-outs are another mechanism for protecting buyers. Often the existing management will continue to work in the business with a deferred consideration payable on performance. Earn-out provisions need to be tailored to the particular situation and should cover:

- The relationship between the seller and the buyer especially when it comes to decision-making
- The length of the earn-out period
- The formula for calculating the earn-out consideration
- Limitations on actions by the buyer to actively depress the profits (or whichever criteria are used to calculate the earn-out)

Earn-outs have a number of advantages for the buyer and a similar number of disadvantages for the seller.

Advantages for the buyer:

- The purchase price reflects performance. Sellers routinely overestimate potential. This is a way of only paying for performance above a certain level
- As the final price is based on future profits an earn-out should ensure the continued commitment of the sellers for at least the earn-out period. This may be particularly important if the target company is dependent on existing management or a single executive
- Unless money is paid into an escrow account, earn-outs enable the buyer to delay payment of a portion of the purchase price

Disadvantages for the seller:

- Although the sellers may be involved in the business after the deal, they will not be in charge of it. The buyer will be able to take all major decisions and the future profitability of the target company may be dependent on matters solely within the buyers control e.g. the provision of finance. The seller therefore only has limited control over profits in the earn-out period and it may receive less under the earn-out than it would expect. This may also create bad relations between the continuing management and buyer
- Payment of part of the purchase price is delayed

- It is easy for sellers to be transfixed by a high maximum purchase price under the earn-out which is based on criteria which in practice will be unachievable given the involvement of the buyer

Disadvantages for the buyer:

- The management team may focus solely on delivering the required numbers to an earn-out target as opposed to taking more of a long-term view
- The business may struggle to adapt to significant market events or opportunities as the structure and agreed expenditure limits reduce its flexibility

Earn-outs are less popular now than they were, mainly due to the drawbacks just outlined. In addition, there is always a difficulty (which can be common with retentions) of establishing whether the relevant criteria have been met. Although the share sale and purchase agreement may contain relatively detailed provisions setting out the accounting policies to be applied and the process for agreeing a set of accounts, it is not uncommon for accountants on both sides to disagree about the precise figures.

If you are going to use an earn-out structure, keep the earn-out period short: one or two years. Also be clear and realistic about commitments and restraints. But remember that about half of acquisitions with an earn-out agreement end in tears.

Representations and warranties

The agreement should provide representations and warranties to the buyer about the company's state and history, including any liabilities, together with indemnities where appropriate. The buyer will also provide representations in the agreement concerning the financial and legal condition of its business. Warranties, and the indemnities that go with them, are such an important part of the contract negotiations that they are dealt with in more detail in the next section. Suffice it to say for now that there are two primary functions of the representations and warranties:

- First, as mentioned in Chapter 5 (Investigating the target), they are an integral part of the buyer's due diligence investigation. Exceptions to warranties are disclosed. The disclosures give the buyer information on the state of the business
- Second, they aid in the allocation of risk between the parties. Generally speaking, the aim is to make the seller liable for liabilities incurred prior to completion and the buyer liable for liabilities incurred after completion

If the representations of a party to the agreement prove to be false before the deal the other party may be able to walk away without incurring liability or, if they turn out not to be true afterwards, the buyer may be able to sue for misrepresentation.

Misrepresentation

A claim for misrepresentation can arise from statements made in pre-contractual negotiations, during due diligence, in the acquisition agreement itself or in the documents disclosed with the disclosure letter. The seller will be particularly concerned to avoid liability for statements made by employees during due diligence as this is an area over which it has little control. The seller will seek to do this by including an 'entire agreement clause' and/or exclusion clause.

An entire agreement clause provides in effect that the buyer has not relied on any representation or undertaking whether oral or in writing save as expressly incorporated in the agreement. By excluding reliance, one of the essential elements of a misrepresentation claim is removed. In the past, however, such claims have not been sufficient in all cases to exclude liability.

If a seller wishes to exclude the possibility of a claim for misrepresentation, the clause must:

- Specifically exclude liability for statements other than those contained in the agreement and the buyer must acknowledge this to be the case
- Distinguish between liability for negligent or innocent misrepresentation, the exclusion of which may be fair and reasonable, and liability for fraudulent misrepresentation, the exclusion of which is unlikely to be either fair or reasonable (according to the Unfair Contract Terms Act 1977)

Restrictive covenants

Following acquisition of the target, the buyer will not want the goodwill it has just bought to be eroded. It will therefore wish to prevent the seller competing against it in the same market. Restrictive covenants are normally inserted in share sale agreements to prevent this. Covenants are agreements by the parties either to do something, or refrain from doing something, for a specified period of time. They impose restrictions on how the parties conduct their businesses prior to closing, describe actions that must be taken to consummate the transaction and prescribe how the parties must respond to third parties, such as other would-be buyers.

Most covenants, especially those of the buyer, expire at closing. Other covenants, such as an agreement by the seller not to compete or not to tempt away the target's employees or customers, usually continue well beyond closing.

This is an extremely complex area of law. An outline of the principles involved is set out below.

Legally speaking, covenants in contracts which restrict a seller's or an employee's activities are considered unenforceable as being contrary to public policy. Two conditions must be fulfilled for them to be valid:

- The restraint must be reasonable and in the interests of the contracting parties, and

- It must be reasonable and in the interests of the public

A restrictive covenant will therefore be unreasonable and void if it extends beyond protecting the legitimate interests of the parties concerned. It is therefore essential to spend time working out exactly what the buyer needs to protect. It is far better to have an enforceable but limited restrictive covenant than a widely-drafted but unenforceable one. Questions to consider include:

- Will the seller have a continuing interest in the same area of business following the deal and if so, where, geographically, will the business continue to operate?

- What is the nature and location of the target's business? Is there likely to be any change in the nature of the business?

- Are there any senior employees of the target who will cease to be employed as a result of the sale who have had contact with valuable customers, potential customers and suppliers? Have they had access to trade secrets/confidential information?

Types of restrictive covenant

Having set out the basics, both sides are in a position to decide what restrictions will be necessary. One or more of the five main types of restrictive covenant discussed below might be needed.

- *Non-competition*. This seeks to prevent the seller from competing in the same business as the target. It will be unenforceable unless it applies only to the existing business and the geographical areas in which the target operates

- *Non-solicitation of customers*. This type of restrictive covenant seeks to prevent the seller from soliciting the custom of the target's customers after completion. The smaller and more clearly defined the group of prohibited clients in the agreement the better

- *Non-dealing with customers*. This type of covenant is broader than the above as it seeks to prevent not just solicitation but dealing with existing customers. Again the more precise the drafting the better the chances of enforcing it

- *Non-solicitation of employees*. This seeks to stop the seller trying to recruit employees of the target after completion. Such covenants are probably enforceable if they only apply to senior employees
- *Confidentiality clause*. This seeks to protect the target's confidential information. The law is more willing to protect secret processes which are vital to the business (i.e. trade secrets) than it is other types of confidential information

Therefore, restrictive covenants must protect a legitimate business interest and must be reasonable in scope, geography and time. They are included in share purchase agreements to protect the goodwill that the buyer is purchasing and are therefore perfectly legitimate at the time the agreement is signed. They must also be reasonable when they are enforced (if they ever are) and be 'wholly' reasonable. For example, if a court considers that a one-year restriction is enforceable but the contract contains a three-year restriction then the whole restriction would be void. The court would not enforce the one-year restriction. It is important that they are drafted specifically for the deal and not just cooked up in a standard form. For this to happen the lawyers drafting them must understand:

- The business
- Why the seller is selling the business (and any problems associated with it)
- Why the buyer is buying the business and where it perceives the business's particular value to be

Definitions

The definitions section defines the terms used throughout the document (where definitions are used in one section only, they are usually found in that section). The most important are the key concepts which actually define how the agreement works. Definitions are usually fairly easy to recognise because they usually start with a capital letter.

Conditions to closing

Certain conditions will need to be satisfied prior to the closing of the transaction. Examples of common conditions include the receipt of regulatory approvals and third-party consents. In most cases, the acquisition agreement provides that if one party fails to satisfy its conditions prior to closing, the other party can walk away.

As a general rule, conditions should be avoided unless they are required by law or are commercially necessary for one or both parties. They fall into two categories, subjective or objective, and can include some or all of those set out in

Table 8.2. Subjective conditions are fine if you are the party in control of the condition but they should be avoided at all costs if you are subject to the whim of the other party.

Table 8.2	Examples of conditions to closing	
	Objective	*Subjective*
Description	These normally depend on third-party actions and can be seen to have occurred e.g. the clearing of a proposed merger by the Competition Commission	These rely on the satisfaction of either the buyer or the seller e.g. the buyer being satisfied about the due diligence it has carried out
Examples	• All relevant notifications and filings made and consents obtained from all authorities e.g. competition authorities and industry regulators	• The buyer must complete satisfactory due diligence
	• Approval of the transaction by the seller's or buyer's board, directors or shareholders • The target's debt being repaid	• The buyer must be satisfied that the seller is the sole legal owner of the shares to be purchased and that no options or other interests exist over those shares or any shares in the target's subsidiaries
	• Loan agreements to fund the acquisition becoming unconditional (other than that the transaction completes)	
	• All consents, approvals and confirmations from third parties obtained and agreements not revoked e.g. in a business where there are a few large contracts, confirmation from the largest customers that a change of control clause will not be invoked	

Consequences of conditions

There are a number of consequences which flow from having conditions:

- *Conduct of the business between exchange and completion.* There will be a period after signature of the sale and purchase agreement before the conditions are satisfied. In this period the seller will be keen to carry on its business without interference by the buyer while the buyer will want to make sure that the business carries on as normal. The usual mechanism is to provide that the buyer will be kept fully informed of all material matters and of any material matters arising which are outside the ordinary course of business. The buyer may also have a veto, or at least a right to be consulted, over any action that is to be taken over such matters

- *Warranties.* Warranties (see below) are given at the time of signing of the sale and purchase agreement. A buyer will normally also want them to be repeated at completion so it is protected against any changes in the target between signature and completion. A seller will usually strongly resist the repetition of warranties. It will argue that risk in the business should pass to the buyer at the time of signing the contract and that as a buyer will get the benefit of any events occurring between signing and completion it should also be prepared to accept any liabilities or losses which occur over the same period

- *Disclosure.* There will be a similar discussion over whether the seller should be permitted to update its disclosure letter at completion. If it is permitted to do so and discloses matters which were not disclosed in the previous disclosure letter the buyer will want a right to rescind the contract

- *Fulfilment of conditions.* The agreement should contain an appropriate long-stop date if conditions are not fulfilled and should also explain what is to occur, when. In particular, the following matters need to be considered:
  - Will both parties bear their own costs?
  - Confidentiality – it is important that all confidential information is returned
  - Poaching of staff and customers. The seller can help prevent this if its employment contracts contain suitably drafted restrictive covenants

Indemnification

The indemnification section is the principal mechanism for the monetary risk allocation in the agreement. It defines the rights of the buyer and seller to be compensated for breaches by the other of the representations, warranties, covenants and other obligations contained in the agreement.

Although the indemnification provisions most often run in favour of the buyer, the seller may also be an indemnified party. For example, in a deal where the purchase price is paid in the common stock of the buyer, the seller often seeks indemnification for false representations regarding the buyer's business and other matters that could impact the value of the buyer's stock.

Warranties and indemnities are covered in the next section.

General

The last section of the contract contains what is often called 'boilerplate'. Boilerplate is a technical legal term describing the clauses towards the end of an agreement which deal with what might be termed the administrative matters. This section will contain clauses on the applicable law, who pays the legal fees for the agreement, how notices under the agreement should be served and when they take effect and the parties' ability to terminate the agreement and the effect of termination.

The buyer and seller usually agree that each will pay its own expenses. Additionally, the buyer will demand that the seller pays its expenses with its own resources and not use those of the company being sold. The provisions at the end of the contract should always be carefully reviewed as they can often hide one or two unexpected traps.

Warranties and indemnities

There is a fundamental conflict between the seller and buyer in any acquisition. The buyer wants a comeback if what it buys is not what it thought it was buying. The seller, however, likes the principle of *caveat emptor* very much as it means the buyer's remedies and its own corresponding liabilities are restricted.

The function of warranties and indemnities in the acquisition agreement is to limit the operation of the principle of *caveat emptor* – buyer beware. They do this in different ways.

What is a warranty?

A warranty provides a guarantee that a particular state of affairs exists. Any breach of this guarantee which affects the value of the acquisition will entitle the buyer to what is effectively a retrospective price adjustment.

What is an indemnity?

An indemnity, on the other hand, is a guaranteed remedy, paid pound for pound, if an event occurs regardless of whether or not the value of the target is affected.

Issues

The relevant issues are:

- The seller's financial position
- The nature and scope of the warranties and indemnities
- The disclosure letter
- Restrictions on when and how a claim can be made
- The minimum level of claim and a ceiling on the amount recoverable
- How to establish breach and make a claim
- The size of damages

Each is dealt with below.

The seller's financial position

Guarantees are only as good as the person giving them. Warranties and indemnities are no exception to that general rule. If the buyer appears flaky or is about to move all its assets to the Bahamas, it would be as well to think of other forms of protection.

A good example of the creativity sometimes required in finding other remedies came in a case where the buyer and seller disagreed about the likely treatment by the tax authorities of group charges. The buyer thought that group charges would be seen as excessive and therefore give rise to an extra tax liability. It was not comfortable relying on a tax indemnity because it thought it very likely that the indemnity would be called and it was not prepared to spend the time and trouble dealing with the inevitable dispute over the validity of the claim. It also knew that the vendor was not in a strong financial position. In the end it was agreed that the target business would be hived off into a new company, leaving the sellers with a corporate shell in which the tax risk remained.

The nature and scope of warranties and indemnities

Warranties in an acquisition agreement are designed to:

- Protect the buyer from nasty surprises by stating – or warranting – that facts or agreements are as they seem

179

- Provide the buyer with protection if they are not
- Force the seller to provide relevant information and be thorough and accurate in the disclosure letter (see below)

Typically warranties are prefaced by a clause such as:

> *The Vendors/Warrantors warrant to the Purchaser that, save as set out in the Disclosure Letter, the Warranties are true and accurate in all respects.*

Warranties are contractual terms. If they are breached, the purchaser can claim for damages for any loss.

A warranty that existing facts are true and accurate is absolute. Even if the warranty is qualified as being 'to the best of the warrantor's knowledge and belief', it is not necessarily robbed of all effect. The courts will impose an objective test of knowledge. The warrantor will be taken to have knowledge of all the information which could reasonably be expected to be available to him. This is even true where a warranty is given for a future state of affairs. The courts have decided that such a warranty should be a guarantee that the forecast of the future has been honestly made and is based on reasonable assumptions.

After completion, if the buyer decides that it has not got what it bargained for, it will have to establish that:

- The complaint constitutes a breach of a specific warranty or warranties which is not excluded by the disclosure letter, and
- The breach has resulted in the business being worth less than the price paid or, in some limited circumstances, that the buyer has suffered an actual loss

This last point is key. It is not enough for the buyer to demonstrate that a warranty has been breached. It must also prove and quantify the loss. In effect this means that the buyer must show that the company is worth less than it paid for it. This is not always easy by any stretch of the imagination as a host of other factors could have had an influence on value by the time the breach is discovered. This is covered in more detail below.

It is the disclosure letter which limits the scope of the warranties and so it is through the disclosure letter as well as the terms of the agreement that the seller will seek to reallocate risk to the buyer.

The disclosure letter

Warranties are statements of fact made by the seller. They are the basis for the buyer claiming damages where it has relied on inaccurate information and ended up out of pocket. For now, however, we want to concentrate on the disclosures made against warranties.

Warranties will be worded along the lines of 'there is no outstanding litigation except for...' For example the warranty might be 'the target company is not involved in any litigation'. If the seller is asked for such statements, but cannot give them, because, for example, there is litigation, it does not amend the warranty but instead discloses the real facts – which are the details of the actual litigation. This is done in a separate letter, called the disclosure letter. By making accurate disclosures to exceptions to the warranties, the seller avoids any liability under the warranties. It all seems a bit roundabout but it works.

The term 'letter' is something of a misnomer. The 'letter' can end up more like a filing cabinet. This is because entire sets of documents or reports can be part of the disclosure. It is a key negotiating tool. It usually goes through a number of drafts, and sellers will delay disclosing for as long as possible. All of this can require buyers to wade through details at the last minute if they do not insist on early and complete disclosure.

Actual, specific, facts must be disclosed. It is not enough for the seller to make the buyer aware of facts which might have enabled it to discover the problem for itself. Nor is it good enough just to disclose the consequences of those facts. In the case of Levison *vs* Farin, the buyers sued over specific warranties, in particular the change in net asset value since the last balance sheet date. The sellers had disclosed that the target's fortunes were declining because of the seller's ill-health. The court decided that this disclosure was not specific enough to constitute disclosure of what was in fact a breach of the 'no material change in net assets' warranty. The seller should have specifically disclosed that there was a breach of that particular warranty.

The case of Eurocopy plc *vs* Teesdale seems to have established that what counts with exceptions to warranties is the actual knowledge of the buyer and not just what is in the disclosure letter. In this case, the sellers had warranted that all material facts had been disclosed. The acquisition agreement also contained the standard clause to the effect that, apart from information set out in the disclosure letter, the buyer's knowledge of the target's business and affairs at completion was irrelevant. Nonetheless, the Court of Appeal ruled that a buyer should not be able to claim that it has suffered loss by purchasing shares at a certain price when, because of breach of a warranty, the shares were actually worth less. As the buyer knew all about the company's problems before it agreed the price it must therefore have taken them into account before deciding how much to pay.

This is a ruling which conflicts with the fundamental principle that it is up to contracting parties to decide what goes into their agreement. It means that buyers should be wary of making claims for breach of warranty for matters about which they clearly have knowledge. Also buyers should certainly not agree that their due diligence constitutes disclosure.

Restrictions on when and how a claim can be made

First, it is best to avoid making a claim. You are unlikely to recover the damages you consider reasonable. You can end up with substantial costs and spend a lot of time on it – all of which is a diversion from running the business. The seller will impose restrictions on the buyer's ability to choose when and how to make a claim. In particular it will insist on:

- Shorter time limits than the statutory six-year period. These are enforceable and generally require any claim to be made within two or three years of completion. Beware, because short time limits can be inappropriate for some types of warranty such as environmental warranties
- Formal requirements for giving notice of the claim. These are likely to be prescribed in the agreement and these must be complied with before the notice is effective. Generally, the notice will have to specify in reasonable detail what gives rise to the claim, the specific breaches that result and the amount claimed

The minimum level of claim and a ceiling on the amount recoverable

Similarly, the seller will want to impose restrictions on the minimum and maximum size of claims as follows:

- *De minimus* provisions, i.e. minimum amounts for the size of claims. This avoids dozens of small claims being made but can have quite expensive repercussions in areas such as employment, where individual claims may be small, but come to a lot if they are all added up. For this reason, *de minimus* claims should be carefully negotiated
- As well as a minimum level of claim, a seller will want a maximum level of claim. The ceiling of liability is often fixed at the amount paid for the target, but it is a matter for negotiation

The quantification of the claim can often be a difficult matter. However, it is important that the buyer is able to maintain a consistent position so that the case set out in the notice will form the basis for litigation if this becomes necessary.

How to establish breach and make a claim

To obtain compensation, an acquirer has to prove that a 'loss of bargain' has incurred due to the seller breaching the warranty. Proving a warranty breach and quantifying the subsequent loss through the courts can be time-consuming and expensive.

The starting point is to identify the specific warranty or warranties under which the claim can be made and then to gather the necessary evidence. A complaint may constitute breach of more than one warranty and it is important that all the possible alternatives are identified at the outset.

The size of damages

The general principle is that the buyer is entitled to the difference between the value of the company or business as warranted and its actual market value. Although this sounds very straightforward and logical, in practice this principle is not always easy to apply.

The purchase price is generally taken as the warranted value and one of the normal commercial methods of valuation is applied to assess the market value. However, the purchase price will not always reflect the warranted value. For example a buyer may have paid an inflated price for reasons of its own. A buyer who overpays will not be able to recover that overpayment in damages. There will also inevitably be a dispute as to the method of valuation to be applied, with each party arguing for the method which produces the most favourable valuation for it.

In some circumstances, a different measure may be adopted. An illustration of the departure from the general rule is the case of Levison *vs* Farin mentioned above. The buyer complained that the net assets of the company were £8,000 less than the warranted value. This did not necessarily mean that the value of the company was diminished by the same amount. The buyer argued that she required £8,000 to put the company into the position it had been warranted to be in. The court accepted the argument and awarded the full amount. In the case of TFL Prosperity the charterers of a ship recovered damages representing the loss of profit resulting from a smaller-than-warranted hold size.

Post-acquisition claims for breach of warranties or indemnities are extremely uncertain. Generally, decisions are made to settle claims at a fairly early stage not least because this, rather than litigation, is the only sensible, commercial, solution. Ironically, often a commercially-sound settlement is more likely to be reached if the matter is approached from the outset as if there will be litigation, but this means that the costs of instructing lawyers, obtaining independent reports and interviewing witnesses will probably all be incurred before settlement negotiations even begin. It may well be that when drafting acquisition agreements the parties should consider at the outset whether Alternative Dispute Resolution, rather than litigation, would be in the best interests of all concerned. An agreement to use mediation or determination by an expert to resolve disputed claims may offer the best solution.

Indemnities

As mentioned above, an indemnity is a guaranteed remedy against a specific liability. An indemnity allows both buyer and seller to adopt a 'wait-and-see' attitude. The most common indemnity is an indemnity against tax liabilities and it is a promise by the seller to meet a particular liability should it arise. Most of what has been said above about warranties also applies to indemnities. Other points to keep in mind are:

- The acquisition agreement needs a provision in it to say whether claims under warranties or indemnities have precedence
- In the event of a claim, consider whether any breach of warranty might also give rise to any breach of indemnity and vice versa and which would produce a more favourable result (if an option is available)
- The taxation implications of money received as an indemnity payment as opposed to damages for breach of contract

Other issues which are relevant to indemnity claims are considered as part of the discussion on warranties.

Post-deal

It is essential that line management is made fully aware of the warranties and the correct procedure in the event of a breach and preferably somebody should be given responsibility for identifying possible warranty and indemnity claims which come to light after completion. The managers running the target post-acquisition are unlikely to have been involved in the details of the deal and as businessmen their typical reaction to a problem is to go out and solve it rather than consider whether it could be the basis for a legal claim.

The statutory limitation period for notifying warranty and indemnity claims is 6–12 years. These periods are commonly amended by negotiation in the sale agreement down to as little as two years for commercial warranties and six years for taxation warranties and indemnities.

Diarising these limitation periods is a vital part of the post-acquisition due diligence procedure. The sale agreement can contain formal notification procedures for dealing with warranty and indemnity claims as well as provisions for resolving claims through arbitration and the acquirer should comply with all relevant procedures in accordance with the sale agreement.

Alternatives to contractual warranties and indemnities

Apart from legal protection in the form of warranties and indemnities, other forms of protection can always be negotiated following adverse due diligence findings. These include:

- Price adjustment
- Retention from the purchase price
- Earn-outs
- Third-party guarantees
- Insurance
- Asset sale rather than a share sale
- Exclusion of certain assets and liabilities from the acquisition
- Rectification of any problems at the seller's cost

Cross-border issues

As already mentioned in Chapter 3 (Preliminary negotiations), cross-border transactions can bring the added complication of whether or not agreements are binding. For this reason parties should determine in the agreement at which point in the negotiations they should be bound.

Conclusion

Negotiating the sale and purchase agreement is the scary, adrenalin-charged part of the acquisition process. Focusing on its main elements and not getting lost in the lawyerly complexities of drafting agreements is enormously helpful for success. Leave the details to the lawyers, which after all is what you are paying them for.

This chapter has summarised those main elements.

Notes

1 An ordinary share is what it says – a share in a company which gets exactly the same dividend and representation rights as any other share. Preference shares carry a fixed dividend and come ahead of ordinary shares in liquidations and dividend payments. Convertible preference shares convert to ordinary shares at preset dates on preset terms. Redeemable preference shares have a fixed repayment date.

2 Taken from 'The Role of Escrows in the M&A Market', Savran, Les and Mazzuca, John, Financier Worldwide, March/April 2003.

Checklist for a financial due diligence investigation

The review period would typically cover the last three years.

History and commercial activities

- Summary of the legal structure and ownership of and any changes since the last annual return
- Brief account of history, locations and nature of business
- Copy of the latest business plan and/or any corporate brochures
- Description of products/services and any other trading activities
- Details of main competitors and market position, including estimated market share and any recent industry surveys
- Details of key customers including terms of trade and an analysis of turnover by customer during the review period
- Details of key suppliers including terms of trade and an analysis of purchases by supplier during the review period
- Particulars of any long-term agreements with customers or suppliers and any other significant agreements, contracts or arrangements with third parties
- Note of alternative arrangements for important supplies which are currently single sourced
- Production methods and techniques and the relative position of the business in relation to the 'state of the art' in the industry in which it operates
- Summary of premises showing locations, facilities/area, tenure and purpose, premises not currently in use and the availability of any spare land or buildings
- Details of any rent payable or receivable and sight of leases or tenancy agreements including details of any onerous lease provisions
- Details of any intellectual property and whether the target has taken steps to protect it

- Details of any litigation
- Copies of all contracts relating to the acquisition or disposal of companies or businesses during the last six years

Organisation structure and employees

- Summary of the management structure and division of responsibilities
- List of directors and senior executives and particulars as to:
  - Previous experience and connection before joining business
  - Formal qualifications
  - Duties throughout the review period
  - Age, years of service and date of appointment to the board, if applicable
  - Current remuneration
  - Pension arrangements
  - Other benefits (e.g. use of company car)
  - Service agreements
  - Directorships of companies that carry on business of any kind with the target or its subsidiaries
- Names of former directors and senior executives who have left during the review period along with reasons for departure
- Analysis of staff by department or function and an indication of staff turnover levels
- Details of key employees and strategies to retain them
- Description of salary/wage structure, terms of employment including holidays, pensions and other benefits, notice period, etc
- Details of recent and imminent salary/wage reviews
- Description of recruitment and training policies
- Names of active trade unions, if any, and number of staff affiliated to each
- Details of any disputes during the review period and current staff relations in general
- Details of relationships with self-employed staff, external consultants, contractors and professional advisers
- Details of any restrictive covenants placed on staff who have recently joined or left the company
- Details of any pension and share option schemes

Accounting policies and audit issues

- Copies of audit management letters for the review period
- Authority from the target's auditors to allow access to their working papers for the review period

Management information and control systems

- Details of the IT systems architecture (including web, ERP and accounting systems), the interfaces between each and the extent to which each is used for the reporting of financial and non-financial operating data
- Details of the back-up and disaster recovery procedures
- Details of the management information reporting procedures, including the consolidation process where applicable
- Details of the budget setting process and results of previous comparisons to actual results
- Summary of the key internal controls in place

Trading results

Where possible the following analyses should be provided on a monthly basis:

- Copies of financial statements produced during the review period including interim and non-statutory accounts, if any
- Analysis of turnover and gross profit by principal product groups, customers and geographic destination for the review period
- Analysis of overheads by nature
- Management accounts and other management information used in monitoring the business for the review period, with a reconciliation to the financial statements
- Details of any special features which have influenced the trading results in any year
- Details of any intragroup or related-party transactions
- Details of any currency exposure and hedging arrangements

Assets and liabilities

The following analyses need only be provided at year ends in the first instance:

- Description of fixed asset capitalisation, revaluation and depreciation policies
- Sight of any recent independent or internal valuations
- Analysis of valuation, cost, depreciation/amortisation and net book value of fixed assets by major category, age and whether owned or leased for the review period
- Details of grants received, capital commitments and any significant capital expenditure anticipated but not contracted for
- Analysis of stock (gross and net of any provisions) by type and age
- Analysis of debtors (gross and net of any provisions) by type and age
- Analysis of creditors by type and age and a description of their repayment bases
- Details of hire purchase, leasing and rental agreements
- Details of loan or overdraft facilities, security provided, interest and repayment terms and any payment clauses stipulated for withdrawing from such agreements
- Details of any warranty liabilities and recent claims history
- Details of any contingent, off-balance sheet financing or other liabilities not covered above

Cash flow

- Cash flow statements for the review period if not included in the financial statements
- An explanation of the major variances in the net cash position over the review period

Financial projections

- Any budgets, forecasts and projections available
- Description of basis on which the projections have been derived and supported evidence where available

Current trading

- Monthly management accounts since the review period
- Analysis of the management accounts in line with that provided for the review period, including a commentary on variances to budget

Taxation

- Tax computations and sight of correspondence covering the review period
- Details of current status of tax computations and disputes with tax authorities
- Analysis of brought forward tax losses and ACT, if any, by date of creation
- Sight of any apportionment clearances which have been obtained
- Summary of the findings of the most recent VAT and PAYE/NIC inspections
- Details of any reconstructions, reorganisations and tax clearances during the review period

Other

- Copies of any circulars to members
- Sight of minute books, other statutory books and of the memorandum and articles of association

APPENDIX B

Checklist for working with advisers

Prepare:

- Discuss the proposed acquisition, and due diligence, with those most likely to be involved in and affected by it
- Make sure everyone who needs to understand is clear about what due diligence is about and the advantages of bringing in advisers and what they are expected to do

Consider:

- Whether to set-up a management team
- Who will prepare and agree the initial brief
- Who will choose your advisers and on what criteria
- Who will be the main contact for the advisers
- How your firm will be kept in touch with the progress of the acquisition/ due diligence process

Brief:

- Set out the firm's aims/mission
- Identify all key issues and potential problems that may arise during the course of the due diligence process and during the course of working with your advisers
- Discuss options with your advisers and set out your initial targets for the advisers
- Propose an initial budget and timescale and discuss additional expenses

Select:

- Compile a criteria checklist for choosing advisers
- Give likely or interested advisers details of your organisation, why you need them and an initial brief
- Ask advisers to submit an initial proposal and estimate for the work

- Check references, if given
- Interview the most promising candidates

Interview:

- Make sure you meet the person/persons who will carry out the due diligence and those that will be your principal contacts
- Discuss:
  - Who will do the work and how many will be involved
  - Their relevant experience
  - The schedule for the job
  - The fee and how it will be paid
  - Estimated costs
  - Whether payments should be linked to completion of specific stages in the work

After the interview:

- Eliminate those not suitable
- Compare strengths and weaknesses
- Compare fees and estimated timescale
- Check any points that are unclear
- Assess genuine interest, commitment and professionalism of those interviewed
- Balance advantages and disadvantages
- Decide which you like and with whom you get on well

Agreeing the final brief:

- Discuss your initial brief and the adviser's proposal and refine final brief
- Agree on the timescale, how fees and costs will be calculated and paid

On appointment:

- Draw up and sign contract with your advisers
- Inform all those that need to know when work will commence and who is to be the main contact for the advisers
- Make arrangements (allocate a person) to provide the advisers with information, equipment, and the space they require

Managing the advisers:

- Keep in close contact with your advisers
- Have regular feedback sessions
- Make sure arrangements for working with your advisers are running smoothly

Receiving the results:

- Decide how you want the advisers to report their recommendations and conclusions to you
- Check its accuracy and conclusions before making it available to others within your organisation
- Assess the outcome
- Consider if you have got what you asked for, in the form you wanted it, and its value to your decision making
- Discuss the report with your advisers and its implications, and negotiate amendments or additions where the report fails to meet the agreed brief

After due diligence:

- Decide if you want further advice or guidance and on what financial basis that might be given
- Approve and implement any specific recommendations

Checklist for legal due diligence

Constitution/ownership/status

- Up-to-date constitutional document
  - Does the corporate vendor have power to sell its shares in target?
  - Are there any restrictions in target's articles to the transfer of shares?
- Details of the authorised and issued share capital
- Details of shareholders (including capacity in which they hold shares and any dissenting or untraceable shareholders)
- Shareholders agreements (if any)
- Organisational chart identifying target's group structure and current directors of each group entity
- Options or encumbrances over target's share capital?
- Are any assets used by target owned otherwise than by target?
- Are any of the target's assets encumbered or other than in its possession?
- Are any of the vendors or persons closely connected to them party to or interested in or entitled to any contracts, loans, intellectual property rights, assets, competitive business or claims of, to, by, against or used by target?

Main contracts

- Copies of all manufacturing joint venture, partnership, agency, distributorship, licensing, supply, franchising, out-sourcing agreements and standard contracts for sale of goods/supply of services
- Is target solvent? Are any insolvency proceedings pending?
- Details of all major customers and suppliers
  - Any adverse change in relationships?
- Copies of all contracts relating to target's sale/purchase of companies/ business/assets in last six years
- Copies of loan/credit agreements and related security/guarantee documentation

- Bank account details and mandates
  - Does the acquisition require bank's consent?
- Details of any major option or right exercisable on change of control of target
- Detail of non-compliance with any contracts
- Is target a party to any non-arm's length arrangement?
- Has target given a guarantee or indemnity of any third party's obligations?
- Are any of target's contracts subject to avoidance under insolvency legislation?
- Any contracts dependent on compliance with British Standards or other special accreditations?

Accounts/financial position

- Audited accounts for last three years
- Any management/internal accounts prepared subsequently
- Other documents relating to the financial/trading position of the target since last accounting date
  - Accountants' report?
- Any material adverse change since date of audited accounts?
- Any bad or doubtful debts?
- Are stocks adequate, excessive, unusable etc?
- Is target's plant and equipment in good condition/does it need replacing?
- Has target received any grant?
  - Is this liable to repayment?
  - Can it be forfeited?
- Any expenses borne by target other than for the benefit of target?

Property

- Schedule of properties
- Purchaser to investigate title or vendor's solicitors to issue certificate of title?
- Copies of all deeds and other documents necessary to prove good title

- Copies of all insurance policies
- Details of any mortgages, charges, leases, tenancies, options, licences, restrictive covenants, easements or other restrictions or rights affecting the properties
- Details of all property outgoings
- Details of any disputes with adjoining owners (actual or pending)
- Surveyors' reports?
- Planning/use restrictions?
- Necessary planning permissions/building regulation approvals obtained?
- Special risks (e.g. mines, flooding, subsidence, landfill, common land, asbestos, deleterious materials, environmental etc)
- Any contingent liabilities under previously assigned leases?

Employment and pensions

- Copies of all standard terms and conditions of employment and details of material deviations
- Identify key employees
  - What is their likely response to the sale?
  - What would be their value to the target post-acquisition?
- Details of all directors' service agreements (in particular salaries, notice periods, restrictive covenants and 'parachute' provisions)
- Details of any bonus/profit sharing/option schemes for directors/employees
- Identify all existing and potential employee claims against target
- Details of all pension schemes (including actuarial valuations)
  - What are employer's obligations?

Intellectual property rights

- Identify all registered IPRs and conduct necessary searches (i.e. Trade Marks Registry, Patents Office)
- Identify all material unregistered IPRs
- Particulars of any licence agreement granted by or to a third party
- Details of any IPR-related disputes (actual or prospective)
- Particulars of all confidentiality agreements to which the target is a party
- Does target trade under any name other than its full corporate name?
  - Is it protected?

Information technology

- Is the processing of any of target's data under the control of any third party?
- Do target's computer systems have adequate capacity for the foreseeable future?
- What disaster recovery plans are in place?
- Is any third-party software subject to appropriate escrow agreements?
- Has target suffered any material breakdowns in respect of its computer systems?
- Does target have adequate backup, security and anti-virus protection?
- Is target properly licensed to use the software it actually uses?
- Is any of target's software subject to a 'time stamp' or 'logic bomb' or 'date field' or similar restrictions?

Taxation

- Details for the last six years of all target/target group tax returns and any prior years still open
- Any intragroup transfer of capital assets in last six years?
- Any tax liabilities incurred since date of last audited accounts other than in the ordinary course of trading?

Miscellaneous

- Any other relevant insurance arrangements (product liability/recall, etc)?
- Any current claims under insurance policies?
  - Are any policies liable to be avoided?
- Particulars of any other existing or threatened litigation or claims
- Contingent liabilities (e.g. product liability, guarantees, maintenance obligation, product returns, liabilities under customer incentives, etc)
- Overseas subsidiaries: what overseas advice is required? What governmental or tax consents are required?

Checklist of published information sources

- Newspapers
- Commercial databases
- News clippings services (McCarthy's etc)
- News services (Reuters, Bloomberg etc)
- General trade directories (Kompass, Kelly's, Key British Enterprises etc)
- Specialised trade directories
- Yellow Pages
- Buyers' guides
- Published market reports (Mintel, Keynote, Frost & Sullivan, Euromonitor etc)
- Brokers' reports
- Trade association handbooks/membership listings
- Trade show catalogues
- Trade magazines
- Government reports and statistics
- Companies House
- Industry regulators
- In-house journals and magazines
- Company brochures and promotional material
- The Internet

- Why are we negotiating?
- Who with – what is their style etc?
- What are our objectives? How are they to be valued/in what order of importance?
- When is it best for us to hold the negotiations? And when do we not want to hold them?
- What should be our negotiating style?
- How high should we pitch our demands?
- What are we prepared to trade?
- What are we not prepared to trade?
- What order should we trade in?
- Who do we need in the team? What are their roles?
- Where do we want the negotiations to take place?
- How much time do we need?
- What assumptions have we made in our planning? How can we check their validity?
- Formalise, value and prioritise both your objectives and theirs
- Make sure you know who their decision maker is (he may not be part of the team)
- Identify the concessions you might offer which offer the maximum benefit to the other side with the least cost to you
- Remember – concessions should always be traded, not donated
- Recognise that a win-win outcome cannot be taken for granted – the other side has to signal acceptance
- Be firm but fair
- Aim high with your aspirations but leave room for bargaining
- Decide your fallback position, beyond which you will not settle under any circumstances

- Calculate and track carefully the mid-point between both sides after each bid
- Select team and allocate tasks carefully
- Plan the opening moments in your mind's eye, to build up confidence and a relaxed approach
- Make sure you have authority to sign the agreement. If you don't have it, get it – the last thing you want is some big shot coming in at the end and changing the spirit of the agreement before he will sign it.

APPENDIX F
Skills checklist for conflict negotiation

1 Don't bargain over positions
2 Separate the people from the problem
   - Pay attention to the relationship
   - Put yourself in their shoes
   - Discuss perceptions
   - Involve them in the process
   - Help save face
   - Recognise emotions
   - Allow them to let off steam
   - Use symbolic gestures
   - Listen actively
   - Speak about yourself
   - Build a working relationship
   - Face the problem, not the people
3 Focus on interests, not positions
   - Ask why? Why not?
   - Recognise multiple interests/human needs
   - Make your interests come alive
   - Acknowledge their interests as part of the problem
   - Put the problem before the answer
   - Look forward, not back
   - Be concrete
   - Be hard on the problem, soft on the people
4 Invent options for mutual gain
   - Separate inventing from deciding
   - Broaden your options/brainstorming
   - Look through the eyes of different experts
   - Invent agreements of different strengths

- Change the scope
- Identify shared interests
- Ask for their preferences
- Make their decision easy – who/what?

5 Use objective criteria
  - Fair standards
  - Fair procedures
  - Joint search for objective criteria
  - Negotiate appropriate standards
  - Never yield to pressure, only to principle

Index